陳式太極扇

冷先鋒　编著

掃碼學習太極扇

YouTube 學習太極扇

Chen Style Taijishan

《國際武術大講堂系列教學》
編委會名單

《陳式太極扇》
編委會名單

序言
武術，源于中國、屬于世界。

　　欣聞學生冷先鋒近期出版發行《陳式太極扇》一書，對此表示由衷的祝賀。其實，早在九十年代初，冷先鋒就追隨我學習各式太極拳競賽套路及傳統套路，學習態度一絲不苟、認真做好每一招的細節動作，近 30 年一直從事武術太極拳的教學，我特別欣賞他做事兢兢業業、持之以恆，非常專心地去做武術太極拳事業，而且為人特別低調、謙虛謹慎，就算到後來他被香港特區政府以《優秀人才入境計劃》引進到香港，都會不間斷的利用網絡請教我各種技術上和教學上的種種困難和經驗，本人親眼目睹和見證了他的一步步腳印和踏踏實實的成長。

　　在眾多學生當中，冷先鋒算是比較年長的，卻經常會以小師弟的身份請教比他年紀小的師弟師妹們，對陈式太極拳的各種套路尤為專注，加上多年來一邊教學一邊不斷學習積累，成就了這本《陳式太極扇》的著作，他系統地從陰陽虛實、身法轉換，眼神和方位等全面地闡述了每一個招式，語言通俗易懂、圖文並茂，就算是業餘愛好者和初學者也能當入門的教程，重要的是還配有英文翻譯，更是外國朋友學習太極拳的福音。

　　中華武術的傳承發展與創新，離不開國家武術主管部門及廣大武術工作者的不懈努力。民族的才是世界的，希望本書的出版，能為武術早日進入奧運，增進各國武術交流，為太極拳的普及與提高盡一份綿薄之力。

　　是以為序。

世界太極拳冠軍　王二平

2021 年 3 月

Preface

Wushu origins from China - Belongs to the world

I am glad to hear that my student, Mr. Leng Xianfeng will publish the book "Chen style taijishan", and sincerely congratulate him. In fact, Mr. Leng Xianfeng followed me to learn various Tai Chi competition routines and traditional routines in the early 1990s. He was meticulous in his study and carefully worked out the details of each movement. He has been engaged in teaching of martial arts and Tai Chi for nearly 30 years. I particularly appreciate his conscientious hard working and perseverance. He is not only very attentive to the martial arts and Tai Chi career, but also very restrained, modest, and cautious. Even though he had been later introduced to Hong Kong by the Hong Kong SAR Government as " Excellent Talent Project '', he has been consulting me via the Internet about various technical and teaching difficulties and experiences. I have witnessed and experienced how he has steadily grown step by step.

He is relatively older among the many of my students, but he used to consult with his younger brothers and sisters as a younger brother. He has been particularly attentive to the various kinds of Chen style Taijiquan and kept learning while teaching for years. His accumulated knowledge and experience enable the completion this book "Chen style taijishan". It systematically elaborates every movement in aspects of transformations of Yin-Yang, emptiness-solidity, body-shifting, eye-looking and positions, etc. There are full of Illustrations in the book. The descriptions in it are easy to understand. It is suitable for both amateurs and beginners as basic tutorial. The important is that it is also translated into English which is the gospel of foreign friends learning Tai Chi.

The inheritance, development and innovation of Chinese martial arts are inseparable from the unremitting efforts of the authorities of national Wushu as well as many Wushu' co-workers.Not only It belongs to our Nation but also to the world. I hope that the publication of this book will make some contributions to accelerate the Wushu entering the Olympic Games, enhance the exchange of Wushu in various countries, and contribute to the popularization and improvement of Tai Chi.

World Taijiquan Champion
Erping Wang
MAR 2021

冷先鋒簡介

　　江西修水人，香港世界武術大賽發起人，當代太極拳名家、全國武術太極拳冠軍、香港全港公開太極拳錦標賽冠軍、香港優秀人才，現代體育經紀人，自幼習武，師從太極拳發源地中國河南省陳家溝第十代正宗傳人、國家非物質文化遺產傳承人、國際太極拳大師陳世通大師，以及中國國家武術隊總教練、太極王子、世界太極拳冠軍王二平大師。

　　中國武術段位六段、國家武術套路、散打裁判員、高級教練員，國家武術段位指導員、考評員，擅長陳式、楊式、吳式、武式、孫式太極拳和太極劍、太極推手等。在參加國際、國內大型的武術比賽中獲得金牌三十多枚，其學生弟子也在各項比賽中獲得金牌四百多枚，弟子遍及世界各地。

　　二零零八年被香港特區政府作為"香港優秀人才"引進香港，事蹟已編入《中國太極名人詞典》、《精武百傑》、《深圳名人錄》、《香港優秀人才》；《深圳特區報》、《東方日報》、《都市日報》、《頭條日報》、《文彙報》、《香港01》、《星島日報》、《印尼千島日報》、《國際日報》、《SOUTH METRO》、《明報週刊》、《星洲日報》、《馬來西亞大馬日報》等多次報導；《中央電視臺》、《深圳電視臺》、《廣東電視臺》、《香港無線 TVB 翡翠臺》、《日本電視臺》、《香港電臺》、《香港商臺》、《香港新城財經臺》多家媒體電視爭相報導，並被美國、英國、新加坡、馬來西亞、澳大利亞、日本、印尼等國際幾十家團體機構聘為榮譽顧問、總教練。

　　冷先鋒老師出版發行了一系列傳統和競賽套路中英文 DVD 教學片，最新《八法五步》、《陳式太極拳》、《長拳》、《五步拳》、《陳式太極劍》、《陳式太極扇》、《太極刀》等太極拳中英文教材書，長期從事專業的武術太極拳教學，旨在推廣中國傳統武術文化，讓武術太極拳在全世界發揚光大。

冷先鋒老師本著"天下武林一家親＂的理念，以弘揚中華優秀文化為宗旨，讓中國太極拳成為世界體育運動為願景，以向世界傳播中國傳統文化為使命，搭建一個集文化、健康與愛為一體的世界武術合作共贏平臺，以平臺模式運營，走產融結合模式，創太極文化產業標杆為使命，讓世界各國武術組織共同積極參與，達到在傳承中創新、在創新中共享、在共用中發揚。為此，冷先鋒老師於 2018 年發起舉辦香港世界武術大賽，至今已成功舉辦兩屆，盛況空前。

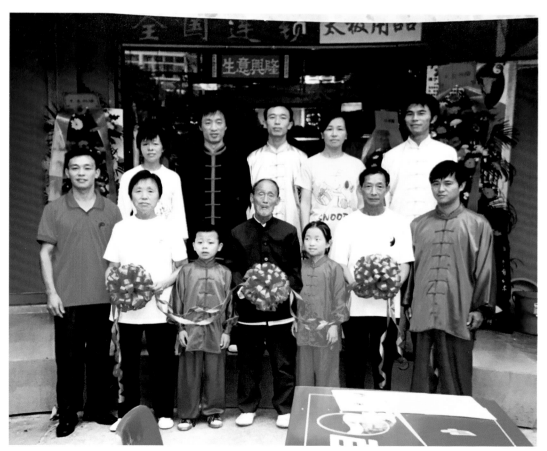

太極世家　四代同堂

Profile of Master Leng Xianfeng

Originally from Xiushui, Jiangxi province, Master Leng is the promoter of the Hong Kong World Martial Arts Competition, a renowned contemporary master of taijiquan, National Martial Arts Taijiquan Champion, Hong Kong Open Taijiquan Champion, and person of outstanding talent in Hong Kong. A modern sports agent, Master Leng has been a student of martial arts since childhood, he is a 11th generation direct descendant in the lineage of Chenjiagou, Henan province – the home of taijiquan, and inheritor and transmitter of Intangible National Cultural Heritage. Master Leng is a student of International Taiji Master Chen Shitong and Taiji Prince, Master Wang Erping, head coach of the Chinese National Martial Arts Team and World Taiji Champion.

Master Leng, level six in the Chinese Wushu Duanwei System, is a referee, senior coach and examiner at national level. Master Leng is accomplished in Chen, Yang, Wu, Wu Hao and Sun styles of taijiquan and taiji sword and push-hands techniques. Master Leng has participated in a series of international and prominent domestic taijiquan competitions in taiji sword. Master Leng has won more than 30 championships and gold medals, and his students have won more than 400 gold medals and other awards in various team and individual competitions. Master Leng has followers throughout the world.

In 2008, Master Leng was acknowledged as a person of outstanding talent in Hong Kong . His deeds have been recorded in a variety of magazines and social media. Master Leng has been retained as an honorary consultant and head coach by dozens of international organizations in the United States, Britain, Singapore, Malaysia, Australia, Japan, Indonesia and other countries.

Master Leng has published a series of tutorials for traditional competition routines on DVD and in books, the latest including "Eight methods and five steps", "Chen-style taijiquan", "Changquan", "Five-step Fist" and "Chen-style Taijijian","Chen-style Taijishan","Taijidao". Master Leng has long been engaged as a professional teacher of taijiquan, with the aim of promoting traditional Chinese martial arts to enable taijiquan to spread throughout the world.

Master Leng teaches in the spirit of "a world martial arts family", with the goal of "spreading Chinese traditional culture, and achieving a world-wide family of taijiquan." He promotes China's outstanding culture with the vision of "making taijiquan a popular sport throughout the world". As such, Master Leng has set out to to build an international business platform that promotes culture, health and love across the world of martial arts practitioners to achieve mutual cooperation and integrated production and so set a benchmark for the taiji culture industry. Let martial arts organizations throughout the world participate actively, achieve innovation in heritage, share in innovation, and promote in sharing! To this end, Master Leng initiated the Hong Kong World Martial Arts Competition in 2018 and has so far successfully held two events, with unprecedented grandeur.

冷先鋒太極（武術）館

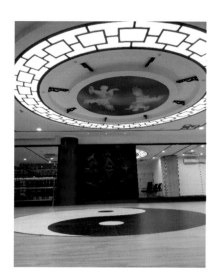

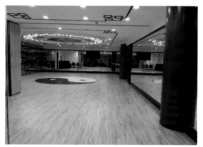

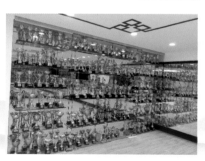

中華武術

火熱招生中......

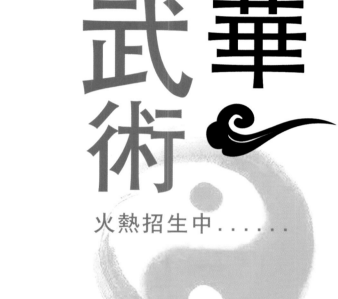

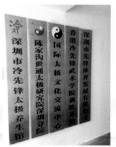

地址：深圳市羅湖區紅嶺中路1048號東方商業廣場一樓、三樓
電話：13143449091　　13352912626

【名家薈萃】

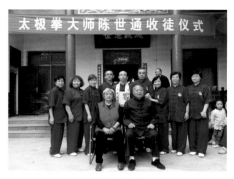

陳世通收徒儀式

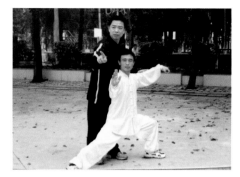

王二平老師

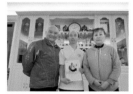

趙海鑫、張梅瑛老師

武打明星梁小龍老師

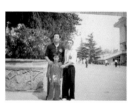

王西安老師

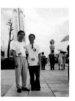

陳正雷老師

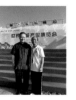

余功保老師

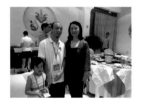

林秋萍老師

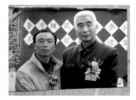

門惠豐老師

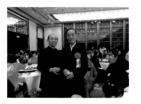

張山老師

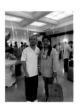

高佳敏老師

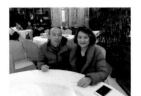

蘇韌峰老師

李德印教授

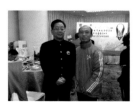

錢源澤老師

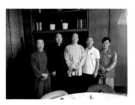

張志俊老師

曾乃梁老師

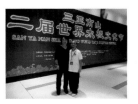

郭良老師

陳照森老師

張龍老師

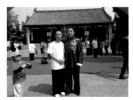

陳軍團老師

【名家薈萃】

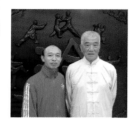
劉敬儒老師

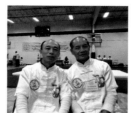
白文祥老師

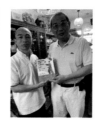
張大勇老師

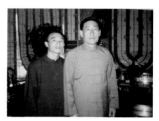
陳小旺老師

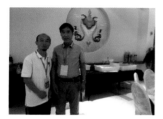
李俊峰老師

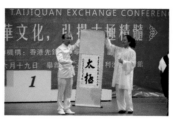
戈春艷老師

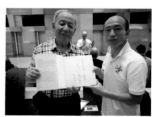
李德印教授

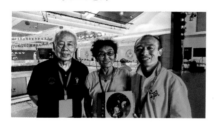
馬春喜、劉善民老師

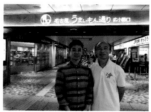
丁杰老師

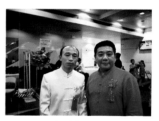
付清泉老師

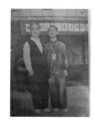
馬虹老師

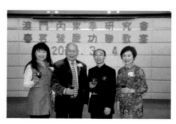
李文欽老師

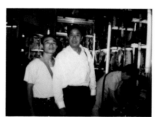
朱天才老師

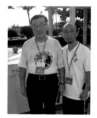
李傑主席

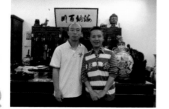
陳道雲老師

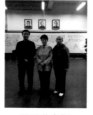
馮秀芳老師

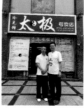
陳思坦老師

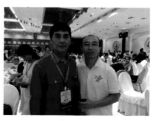
趙長軍老師

【獲獎榮譽】

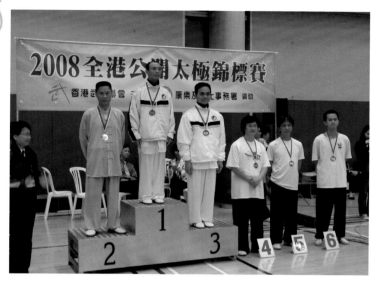

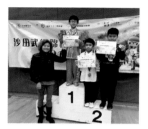

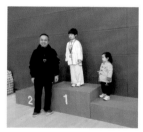

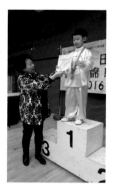

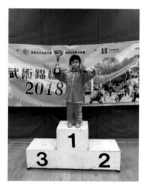

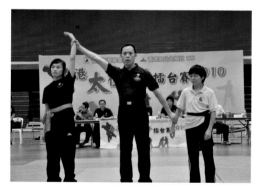

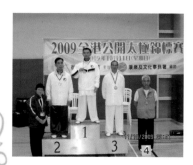

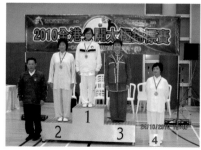

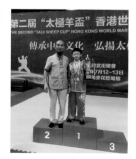

【電視采訪】

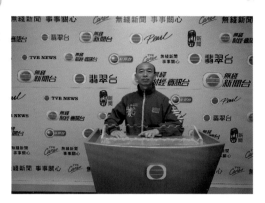
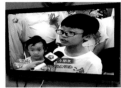
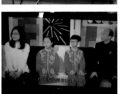
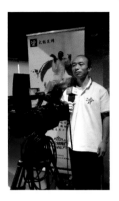
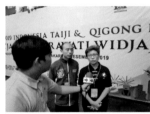
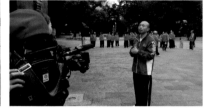
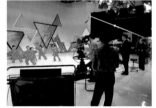
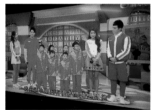
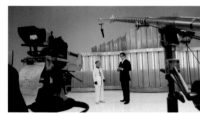
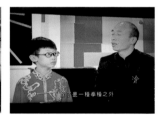
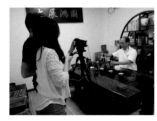
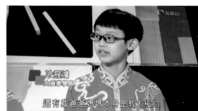
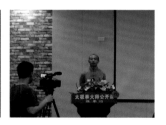
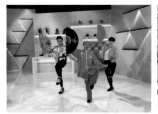
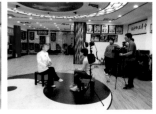
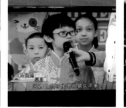
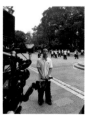

【電臺訪問】

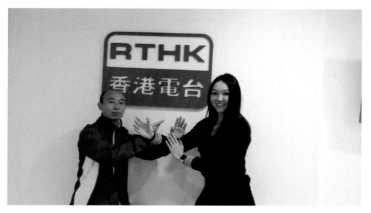

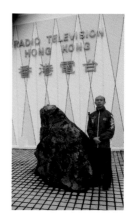

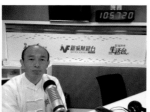

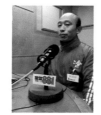

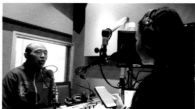

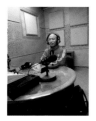

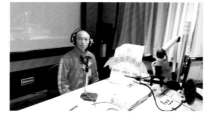

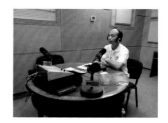

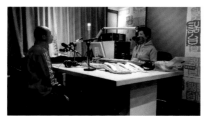

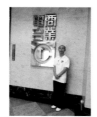

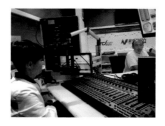

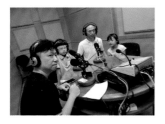

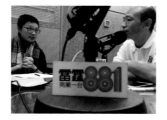

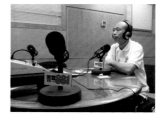

【合作加盟】

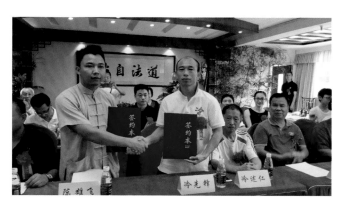

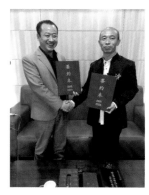

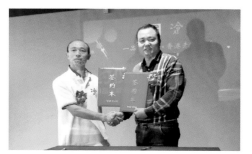

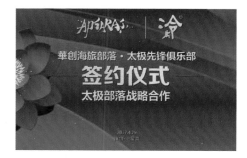

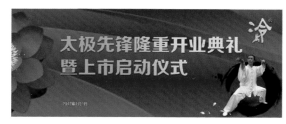

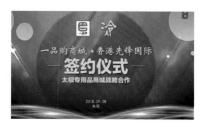

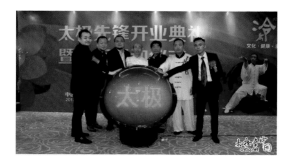

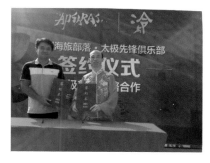

【媒體報道】

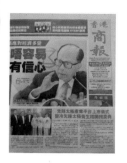
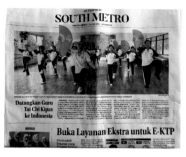
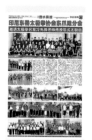
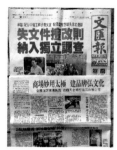

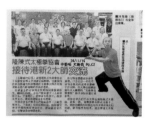
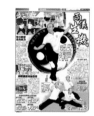
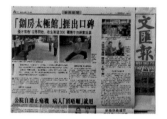
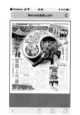

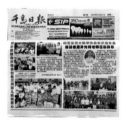
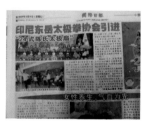
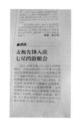
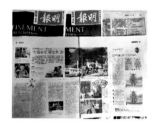

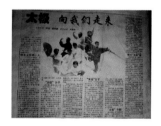
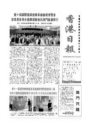
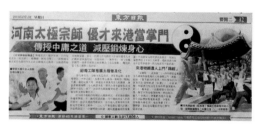

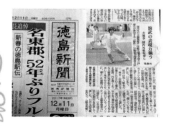
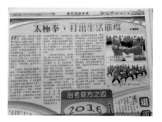
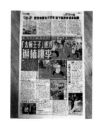
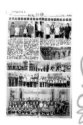

【培訓瞬間】

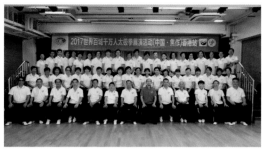
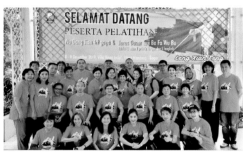

百城千萬人太極拳展演活動 雅加達培訓

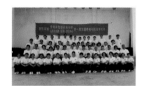
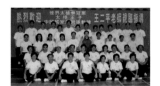
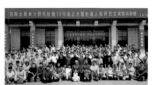

汕頭培訓 王二平深圳培訓 師父70大壽

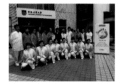
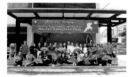
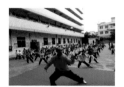
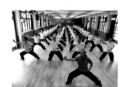

香港公開大學培訓 印度尼西亞培訓 松崗培訓 香港荃灣培訓

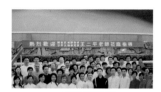
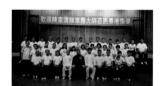
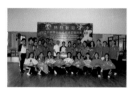

王二平深圳培訓 陳軍團香港講學 印尼泗水培訓

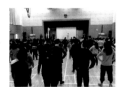
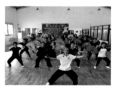
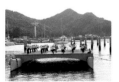
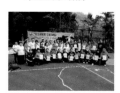

油天培訓 印尼扇培訓 七星灣培訓 陳軍團香港講學培訓

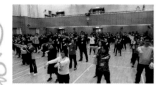
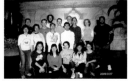
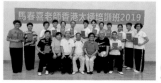

油天培訓 美國學生 馬春喜香港培訓班

【賽事舉辦】

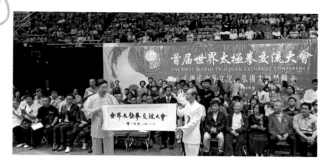

首屆世界太極拳交流大會

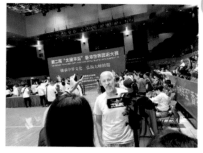

第二屆"太極羊杯"香港世界武術大賽

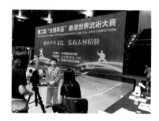

第二屆"太極羊杯"大賽

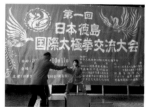

日本德島國際太極拳交流大會

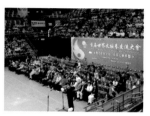

首屆世界太極拳交流大會

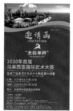

馬來西亞武術大賽

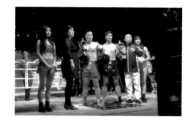

東莞擂臺表演賽

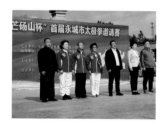

首屆永城市太極拳邀請賽

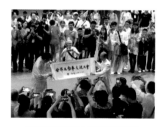

首屆永城市太極拳邀請賽

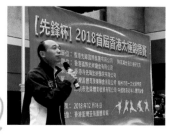

2018首屆香港太極錦標賽

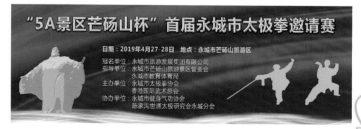

2019首屆永城市太極拳邀請賽

目　　錄
DIRECTORY

1. 第一式　起勢 .... (22)
Opening form

2. 第二式　金剛搗碓 .... (24)
Guardian Pounds Mortar

3. 第三式　攬紮衣 .... (30)
Fasten coat

4. 第四式　六封四閉 .... (33)
Six Sealing and Four Closing

5. 第五式　單鞭 .... (41)
Single Whip

6. 第六式　前招 .... (44)
Forward trick

7. 第七式　後招 .... (45)
Backward trick

8. 第八式　白鶴亮翅 .... (46)
White Crane Flashes its Wings

9. 第九式　斜行拗步 .... (49)
Oblique Stance with Twist Step

10. 第十式　提收 .... (52)
Lift and retract

11. 第十一式　雲手 .... (55)
Cloud Hands

12. 第十二式　掩手肱捶 .... (60)
Hide Hand and Strike with Fist

13. 第十三式　穿心肘 .... (65)
Pierce Elbow

14. 第十四式 摆莲腳 .... (68)
　　Lotus Kick

15. 第十五式 雀地龍 .... (69)
　　Dragon Dives to Ground

16. 第十六式 金鷄獨立 .... (70)
　　Golden Rooster Stands on one Leg

17. 第十七式 翻花舞袖 .... (72)
　　Turn over flowers and flip sleeves

18. 第十八式 海底翻花 .... (74)
　　Flip the ocean waves

19. 第十九式 二起腳 .... (75)
　　jump with double kicks

20. 第二十式 雙震腳 .... (77)
　　Thuds with both feet

21. 第二一式 玉女穿梭 .... (79)
　　Jade Maiden Working Shuttles

22. 第二十二式 當頭炮 .... (81)
　　cannon attack

23. 第二十三式 金剛搗碓 .... (83)
　　Guardian Pounds Mortar

24. 第二十四式 收勢 .... (87)
　　Closing form

注釋： 〇 ❚ 白：代表左腳，黑：代表右腳

⟩ ● 表示前腳掌着地。

∪ ❚ 表示腳跟着地。

○ ● 表示其中一只腳懸空的動作。

————————————▶
代表右手右腳路綫

- - - - - - - - - ▶
代表左手左腳路綫

（一）起勢
1.Opening form

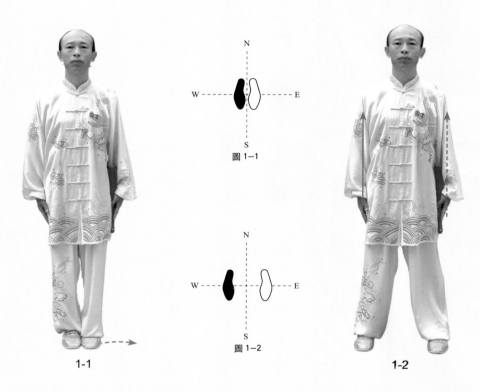

圖 1—1

圖 1—2

1-1

1-2

1 身體自然直立，兩手鬆垂輕貼大腿外側，左手握扇，目視正前方（圖 1—1）；

a. Stand upright naturally, arms relaxed with palms resting lightly on outside of thighs, hold the fan with the left hand, looking straight ahead (Fig.1-1).

2 左腳向左橫開一步，與肩同寬，目視前方（圖 1—2）；

b. Move the left foot one step to the left, shoulder- width apart, looking straight ahead (Fig.1-2).

（一）起勢
1.Opening form

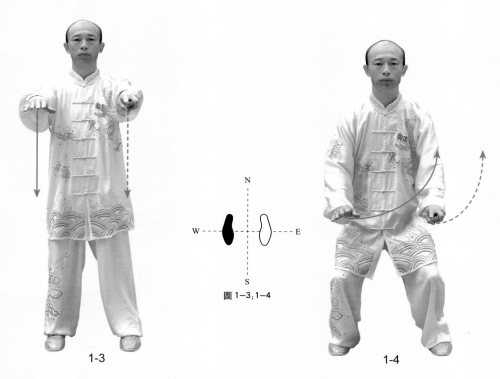

圖 1-3；1-4

3 兩臂向前、向上慢慢平舉，與肩同高，力點在兩手前臂（圖 1-3）；

c. Raise arms slowly forwards and upwards to shoulder-level, the point of force at both forearms (Fig.1-3).

2 屈膝鬆肩鬆胯，兩手向下按掌，微微坐腕，力達掌根，目視前下方（圖 1-4）。

d. Bend knees, relax shoulders, relax hips, press down both palms, bending slightly the wrists, the point of force reaching at bases of the palms, looking forwards and down (Fig.1-4).

（二）金剛搗碓

2.Guardian Pounds Mortar

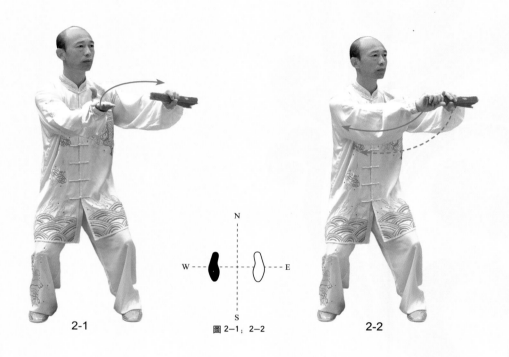

2-1

圖 2-1；2-2

2-2

1 身體左轉，重心微偏右，兩臂向左掤出，掌心朝外，與肩同高，力達掌根，目視左前方（圖 2-1）；

a. Turn the body to the left, shift the body weight slightly to the right, ward off the arms to the left, the palms facing outwards, at shoulder-level, the point of force reaching at the bases of the palms, looking forwards to the left (Fig.2-1).

2 右手內旋，握扇，目視兩手方向（圖 2-2）；

b. Rotate the right palm inwards, hold the fan, looking in direction of the hands (Fig.2-2).

（二）金剛搗碓

2.Guardian Pounds Mortar

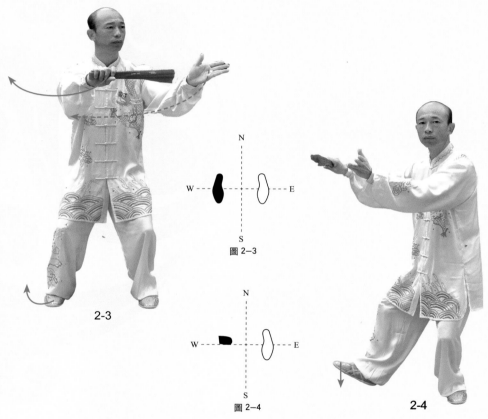

圖 2—3

2-3

圖 2—4

2-4

3 身體右轉，重心左移，兩臂螺旋向右平捋，掌心向外，同時右腳尖外擺，目視兩掌方向（圖 2—3；2—4）；

c.Turn the body to the right, shift the body weight to the left, pull the palms spirally and levelly to the right, the palms facing outwards, at the same time, swing the right toes outwards, looking in direction of the hands (Fig.2-3;2-4).

（二）金剛搗碓

2.Guardian Pounds Mortar

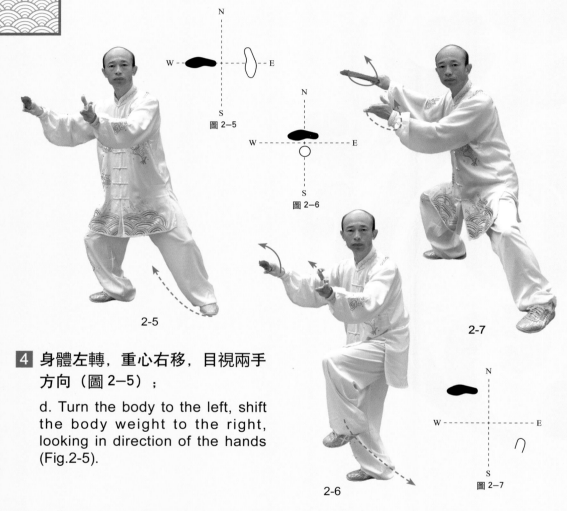

圖 2-5

圖 2-6

2-5

2-6

2-7

圖 2-7

---

4 身體左轉，重心右移，目視兩手方向（圖 2-5）；

d. Turn the body to the left, shift the body weight to the right, looking in direction of the hands (Fig.2-5).

5 提左腳向左前方擦出，同時兩手向右後方平推，目視左腳方向（圖 2-6、2-7）；

e. Lift the left foot and slide forwards to the left, at the same time, push the hands flatly backwards to the right, looking in direction of the left foot (Fig.2-6,2-7).

（二）金剛搗碓

2. Guardian Pounds Mortar

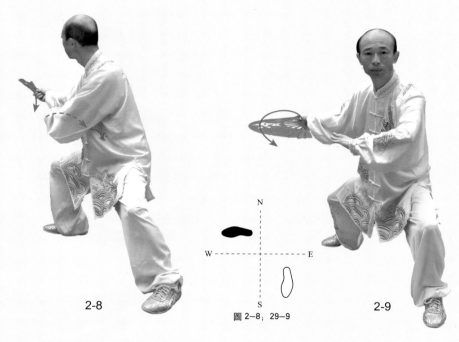

2-8

圖 2-8；29-9

2-9

---

6 身體左轉再右轉，重心左移再右移，兩手順時針旋轉，目視兩手方向（圖 2-8）；

f. Turn the body to the left, then to the right, shift the body weight to the left, then to the right, rotate the palms clockwise, looking in direction of the hands (Fig.2-8).

7 身體左轉，重心左移，左手屈肘向前頂肘，同時右手開扇，目視左前方（圖 2-9）；

g. Turn the body to the left, shift the body weight to the left, bend the left elbow and jab it forwards, at the same time, the right hand opens the fan, looking forward to the left(Fig.2-9).

（二）金剛搗碓

2.Guardian Pounds Mortar

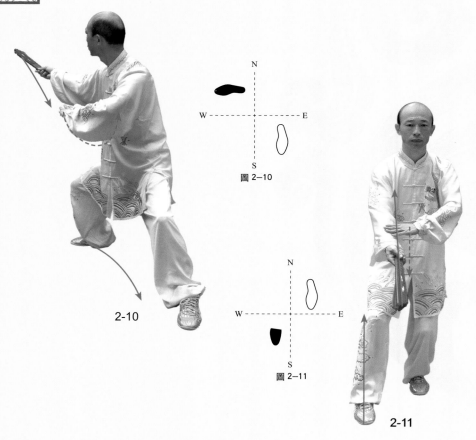

圖 2-10

2-10

圖 2-11

2-11

8 右腳走內弧向前上步，腳尖點地成虛步，同時左手向前撩掌，收扇，右手隨右腳向前和左掌相搭，左掌搭於右前臂，目視右掌方向（圖 2-10；2-11）；

h. Step the right foot forward in an inward arc, resting on tips of toes to form an empty stance, at the same time, flick the left palm forwards,close the fan,flick the right hand forward to meet with the left palm, the left palm rests on the right forearm, looking in direction of the right palm (Fig.2-10；2-11).

（二）金剛搗碓

2.Guardian Pounds Mortar

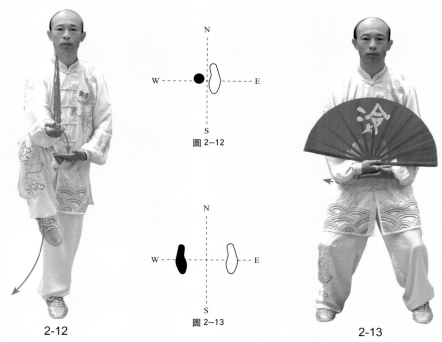

圖 2—12

圖 2—13

2-12

2-13

9 右手開扇上舉，與鼻同高，左掌收至腹前，掌心向上，同時提右膝，高過水平，腳尖下垂，目視前方（圖 2–12）；

i. Open the fan with the right hand, then raise it to nose-level, move the left palm to in front of the abdomen, palm facing up, at the same time, lift the right knee, higher than level, toes facing down, looking straight ahead (Fig.2-12).

10 右腳下震，與肩同寬，重心偏左腳，兩腳平行，同時右手砸於左掌上，目視前方（圖 2–13）。

j. Drop the right foot with a thud, shoulder- width apart, the body weight slightly to the left, feet parallel, at the same time, pound the back of the right hand onto the left palm, looking straight ahead (Fig.2-13).

（三）攬紮衣
3.Fasten coat

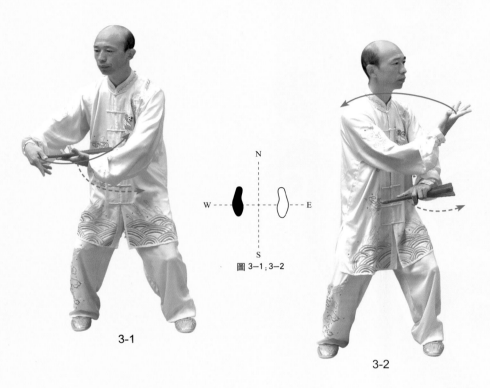

3-1

圖 3-1；3-2

3-2

1 身體微右轉再左轉，重心先右移再左移，先收扇換左手握扇，右掌從左臂內側上穿，目視右手方向（圖 3-1、3-2）；

a. Turn the body slightly to the right, then to the left, shift the body weight first to the right, then to the left, close the fan, then change the left hand to hold the fan, pierce the right palm upwards from the inside of the left palm, looking in direction of the right hand (Fig.3-1, 3-2).

（三）攬紮衣
3.Fasten coat

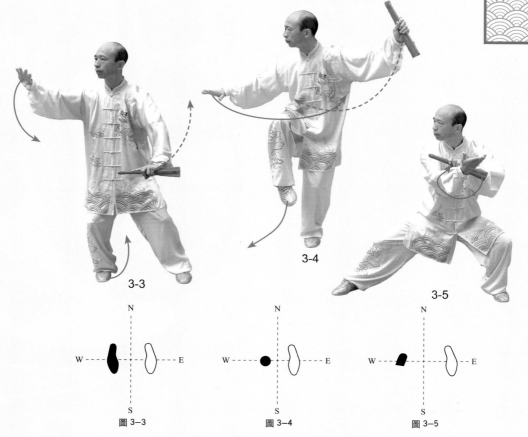

3-3

3-4

3-5

圖 3-3　　　　　圖 3-4　　　　　圖 3-5

2 身體右轉，重心右移，兩手劃弧分開，目視右掌方向（圖 3-3）；

b. Turn the body to the right, shift the body weight to the right, separate both palms in an arc, looking in direction of the right palm (Fig.3-3).

3 身體右轉，重心左移，提右腳向右擦腳，同時兩臂劃弧相合，右臂在外，目視右腳方向（圖 3-4、3-5）；

c. Turn the body to the right, shift the body weight to the left, lift the right foot and slide out to the right, at the same time, draw arms an arc to close together, the right arm at the outside, looking in direction of the right foot (Fig.3-4, 3-5).

（三）攬紮衣
3.Fasten coat

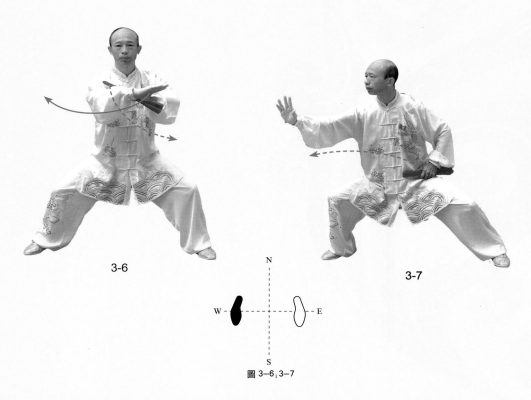

3-6

3-7

圖 3-6；3-7

4 身體右轉，重心右移，兩臂逆時針旋轉，右掌內旋向右橫拉，立掌，力達掌根，同時左手外旋收至腰間，成右偏馬步，目視右掌方向（圖 3-6、3-7）。

d. Turn the body to the right, shift the body weight to the right, rotate both arms counterclockwise, rotate the right palm inwards and pull horizontally to the right, turn palm upright, the point of force reaching at the base of the palm, at the same time, rotate the left palm outwards to the waist, shift the body weight to the right, adopt a right-biased horse stance, looking in direction of the right palm (Fig.3-6, 3-7).

（四）六封四閉
4.Six Sealing and Four Closing

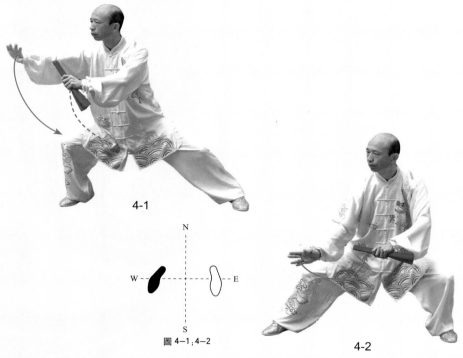

4-1

圖 4—1；4—2

4-2

1 身體右轉，重心左移再右移，同時左手向右推掌至右手腕內下側，目視右掌方向（圖 4—1）；

a. Turn the body to the right, shift the body weight to the left, then to the right, at the same time, push the left palm to the right to the lower inside of the right wrist ,looking in direction of the right palm (Fig.4-1).

2 身體左轉，重心左移，同時右掌外旋、左手內旋，向左向下捋帶，目視右掌方向（圖 4—2）；

b.Turn the body to the left, shift the body weight to the left, at the same time, rotate the right palm outwards and the left arm inwards, pull downwards to the left, looking in direction of the right palm (Fig.4-2).

（四）六封四閉

4.Six Sealing and Four Closing

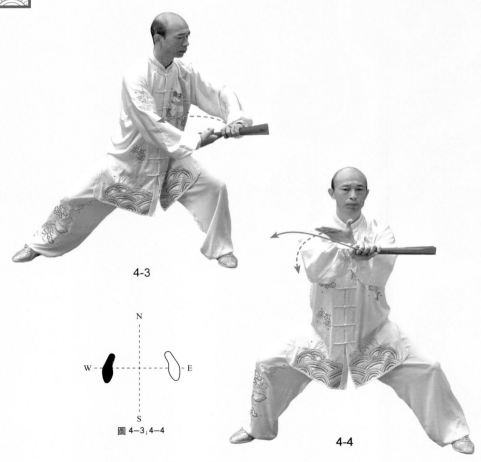

4-3

圖 4-3；4-4

4-4

3 身體繼續左轉，右手握扇，兩手相合，手背相對，目視兩手方向（圖 4-3；4-4）；

c. Without stopping, turn the body to the left, hold the fan with the left hand , palms come together, back to back,looking in direction of the hands(Fig.4-3;4-4).

（四）六封四閉
4.Six Sealing and Four Closing

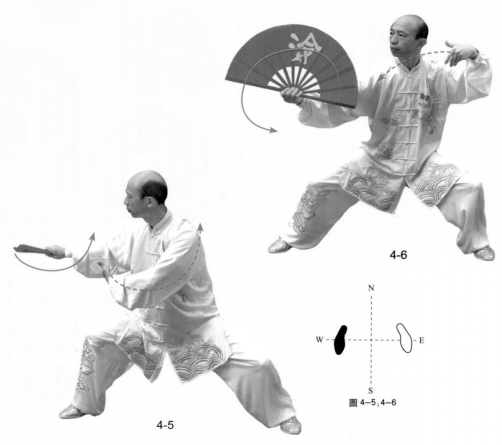

4-6

4-5

圖 4-5；4-6

4 身體右轉再左轉，重心右移再左移，兩手劃弧向右、向下，再向左、向上開扇，同時左手變刁手收至左耳側，目視扇的方向（圖 4-5；4-6）；

d. Turn the body to the right, then to the left, shift the body weight to the right, then to the left, draw both hands in an arc to the right, downwards, then to the left, upwards and open the fan, at the same time, grip the left hand in a hook to the side of the left ear, looking in direction of the fan (Fig. 4-5, 4-6).

（四）六封四閉

4.Six Sealing and Four Closing

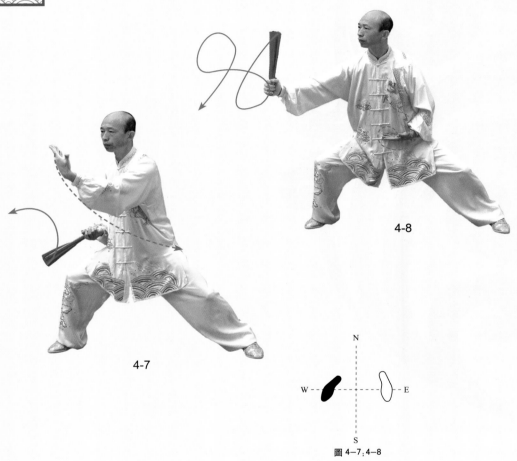

4-8

4-7

圖 4-7；4-8

5 身體右轉，右手外旋收扇，劃弧向右前方推出，同時左手劃弧收至腹前，目視扇的方向（圖 4-7）；

e. Turn the body the right, rotate the right hand outwards and close the fan, then draw in an arc and push forwards to the right, at the same time, draw the left hand in an arc to in front of the abdomen, looking in direction of the fan (Fig. 4-7).

（四）六封四閉
4.Six Sealing and Four Closing

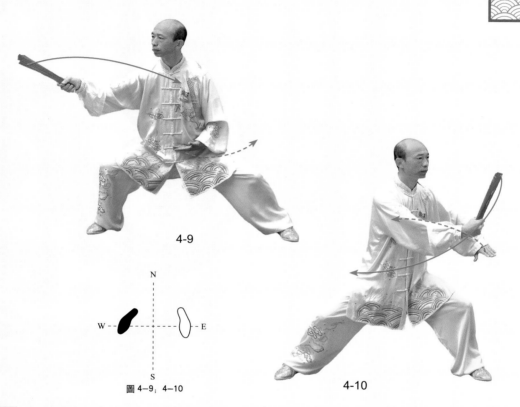

4-9

图 4—9；4—10

4-10

6 右手内旋再外旋，成 8 字軌迹，向前下點扇，目視扇的方向（圖 4—8；4—9）；

f. Rotate the right hand inwards, then outwards to make an 8-character track, point the fan forwards and downwards, looking in direction of the fan (Fig.4-9).

7 身體左轉，重心左移，右手握扇向左劃弧，同時左手向左摟膝至左胯旁，目視扇的方向（圖 4—10）；

g. Turn the body to the left, shift the body weight to the left, at the same time, the right hand holds the fan and draw in an arc to the left, the left hand blocks to the left, bypassing the front of the left knee to the side of the left hip, looking in direction of the fan (Fig. 4-10).

（四）六封四閉

4.Six Sealing and Four Closing

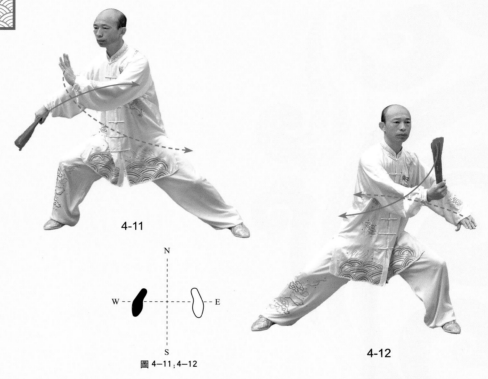

4-11

4-12

圖 4—11；4—12

8 身體右轉，重心右移，右手握扇向右劃弧至右胯旁，同時左手向右劃弧，目視左掌（圖 4—11）；

h. Turn the body to the right, shift the body weight to the right, hold the fan with the right hand and draw in an arc to the right to the side of the right hip, at the same time, draw the left hand in an arc to the right, looking at the left palm (Fig.4-11).

9 身體左轉，重心左移，右手握扇向左劃弧，同時左手向左摟膝至左胯旁，目視扇的方向（圖 4—12）；

i. Turn the body to the left, shift the body weight to the left, hold the fan with the right hand and draw in an arc to the left, at the same time, the left hand blocks to the left, bypassing the front of the left knee to the side of the left hip, looking in direction of the fan (Fig.4-12).

（四）六封四閉
4. Six Sealing and Four Closing

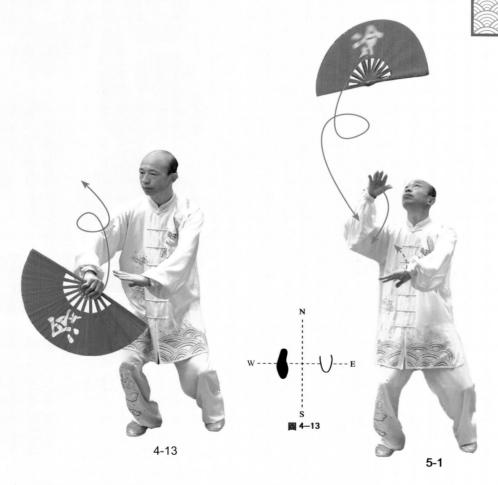

4-13

圖 4-13

5-1

10 身體右轉，重心右移，右手開扇，同時左腳收至右腳內側，腳尖點地成虛步，
目視扇的方向（圖 4-13）。

j. Turn the body to the right, shift the body weight to the right, open the fan
with the right hand, at the same time, move the left foot to the inside of the
right foot, resting on the tips of the toes to form an empty stance,
looking in direction of the fan (Fig.4-13).

（五）單鞭

5. Single whip

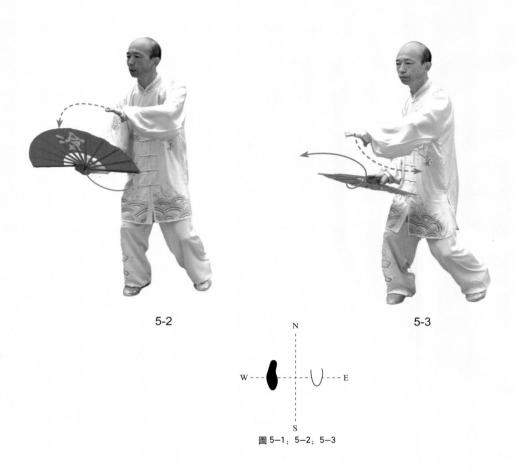

5-2

5-3

圖 5–1；5–2；5–3

1 拋扇，身體右轉，左掌向右前推出，右手翻扇回收，目視左掌方向（圖 5–1、5–2、5–3）；

a. Throw fan, turn the body to the right, push the left palm forwards to the right, with the right hand throw the fan upwards, flipping then catch it, looking in direction of the left palm (Fig.5-1、5-2、5-3).

（五）單鞭

5. Single whip

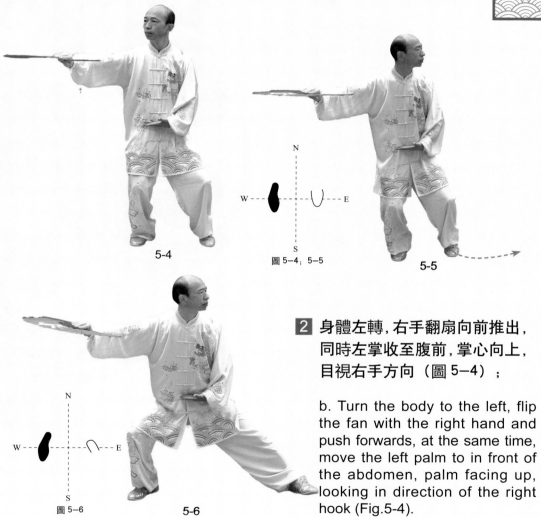

5-4

圖 5-4；5-5

5-5

5-6

圖 5-6

2 身體左轉，右手翻扇向前推出，同時左掌收至腹前，掌心向上，目視右手方向（圖 5-4）；

b. Turn the body to the left, flip the fan with the right hand and push forwards, at the same time, move the left palm to in front of the abdomen, palm facing up, looking in direction of the right hook (Fig.5-4).

3 右腳屈膝，提左腳向左擦出，目視左腳方向（圖 5-5、5-6）；

c. Bend the right knee, lift the left foot and slide out to the left, looking in direction of the left foot (Fig.5-5、5-6).

5

（五）單鞭
5．Single whip

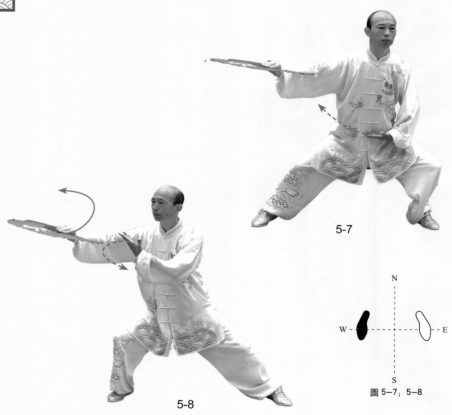

5-7

5-8

圖 5-7；5-8

4 身體左轉，重心左移，襠走下弧，目視前方（圖5-7）；

d. Turn the body to the left, shift the body weight to the left, dip pelvis in a downward arc, looking straight ahead (Fig.5-7).

5 身體右轉，重心右移，左掌向右手方向穿出，目視左掌方向（圖5-8）；

e. Turn the body to the right, shift the body weight to the right, thread through the left palm in direction of the right hand, looking in direction of the left palm (Fig.5-6).

（五）單鞭
5.Single whip

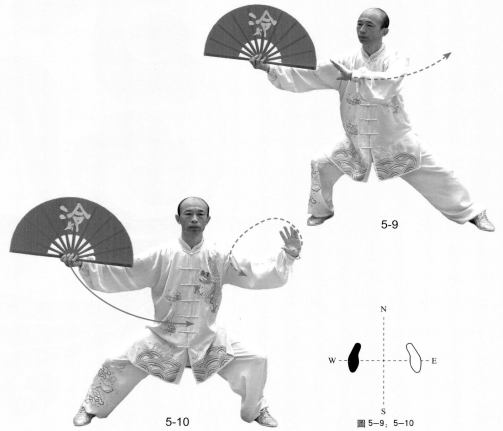

5-9

5-10

圖 5-9；5-10

6 身體左轉，重心左移，同時左掌內旋，向左橫拉，立掌，右手翻轉，立扇，成左偏馬步，目視前方（圖 5-9、5-10）。

f. Turn the body to the left, shift the body weight to the left, at the same time, rotate the left palm inwards, pull horizontally to the left, turn the palm upright, flip the right hand, and turn the fan upright, adopt a left-biased horse stance, looking straight ahead (Fig.5-7.5-8).

（六）前招
6.Forward trick

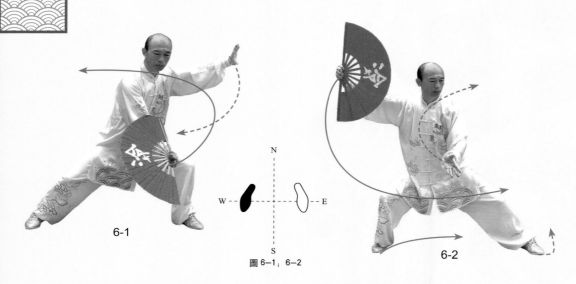

6-1

6-2

圖 6-1、6-2

1 身體左轉再右轉，兩手順時針旋轉，目視右手方向（圖6-1、6-2）；

a.Turn the body to the left, then to the right, rotate arms clockwise, looking in direction of the right palm (Fig.6-1、6-2).

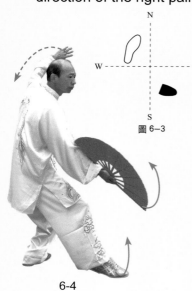

圖 6-3

6-4

2 身體左轉，重心左移，左腳尖外擺，同時右臂外旋至右膝上方，掌心向上，左臂內旋劃弧至左額斜上方，掌心向外，右腳走內弧向前上步，腳尖點地成虛步，目視右手方向（圖6-3）；

c. Turn the body to the left, shift the body weight to the left, the left toe swings outwards, at the same time, rotate the right arm outwards to above the right knee, palm facing up, rotate the left arm in an arc inwards to the upper front of the left forehead, palm facing outwards, step the right foot forward in an inward arc, resting on the tips of the toes to form an empty stance, looking in direction of the right hand (Fig.6-3).

（七）後招

7.Backward trick

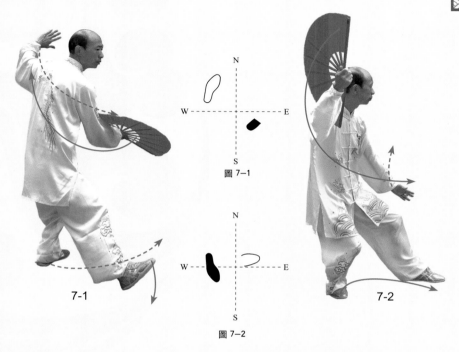

7-1

圖 7−1

7-2

圖 7−2

1 右腳向右前方上步，同時兩臂隨腰向左旋轉，目視右手方向（圖 7−1）；

a. Step the right foot forwards to the right, at the same rotate both arms with waist to the left, looking in direction of the right hand (Fig.7-1).

2 重心移至右腳，左腳提起再腳尖點地成虛步，同時兩臂隨腰向右旋轉，同時左手外旋至左膝上方，掌心向上，右手內旋收至右額斜上方，目視左手方向（圖 7−2）。

b. Shift the body weight onto the right foot, lift the left foot, then resting on the tips of the toes to form an empty stance, at the same time, both arms rotate with the waist to the right, at the same time, rotate the left palm outwards to above the left knee, palm facing up, rotate the right palm inwards to the upper front of the right forehead, looking in direction of the left hand (Fig.7-2).

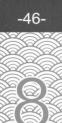

（八）白鶴亮翅

8.White Crane Spreads its Wings

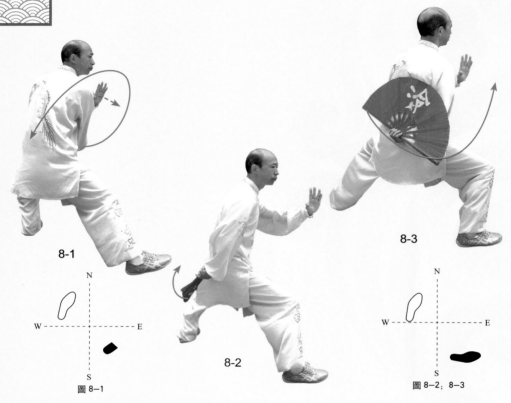

8-1

8-2

8-3

圖 8-1

圖 8-2；8-3

1 身體左轉，提右腳，向右前方擦出，兩臂相合，右臂在下，目視右腳方向（圖 8-1）；

a. Turn the body to the left, lift the right foot, slide forwards to the right, arms come together, the right arm below the left one, looking in direction of the right foot(Fig.8-1).

2 身體右轉再左轉，重心左移再右移，右手經右耳側劃弧至身后，轉腰發力開扇，同時左手劃弧向右推掌，目視左手方向（圖 8-2；8-3）；

b. Turn the body to the right, then to the left , shift the body weight to the left, then to the right, rotate the right palm in an arc through the side of the right ear to the rear, looking in direction of the left hand(Fig.8-2;8-3).

（八）白鶴亮翅
8.White Crane Spreads its Wings

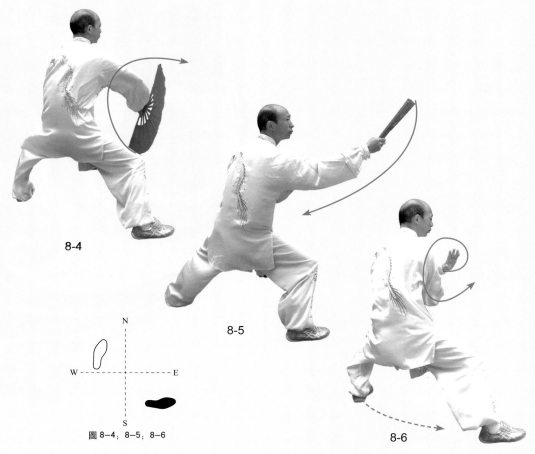

8-4

8-5

8-6

N

W — — — — — E

S

圖 8－4；8－5；8－6

3 身體繼續左轉，右手合扇，順時針劃弧與左臂相合，目視右前方。（圖：8－4；8－5；8－6）；

c. Without stopping, turn the body to the left, close the fan with the right hand, and rotate clockwise to meet with the left arm, looking forwards to the right(Fig.8-4;8-5;8-6).

（八）白鶴亮翅
8.White Crane Spreads its Wings

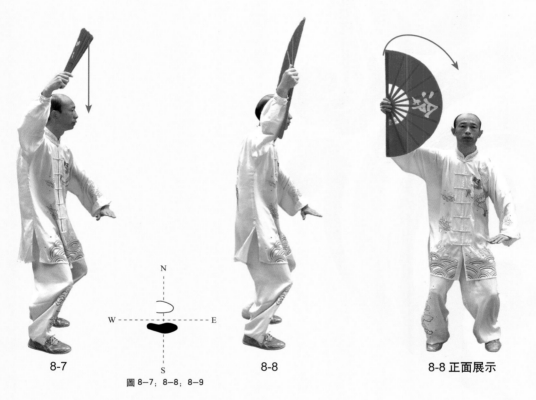

8-7

8-8

8-8 正面展示

圖 8−7；8−8；8−9

4 身體左轉再右轉，重心右移，兩臂逆時針旋轉再上下斜分，右手開扇至右額斜上方，左掌收至左膝上方，掌心向下，同時左腳收至右腳內側，成虛步，目視前方（圖 8−7；8−8）；

d. Turn the body to the left, then to the right, shift the body weight to the right, rotate arms counterclockwise and separate respectively up and down, open the fan with the right hand to the upper right of the forehead, draw left palm to above the left knee, palm facing down, at the same time, move the left foot to the inside of the right foot, adopt an empty stance, looking straight ahead(Fig.8-7;8-8).

（九）斜行拗步

9.Oblique Stance with Twist Step

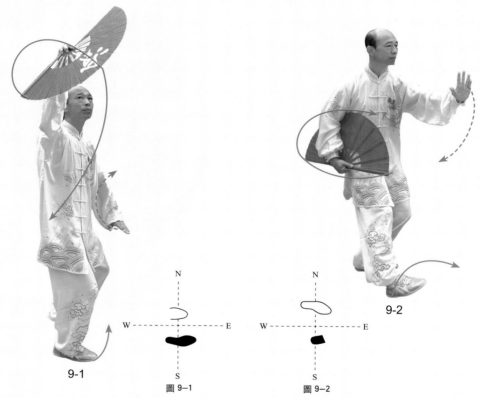

9-1

9-2

圖 9—1   圖 9—2

1 身體右轉、左轉再右轉，右手握扇內旋再收至右腰側，同時左掌隨轉腰向右前推出，重心移至左腳，右腳尖上翹，目視左掌方向（圖 9—1；9—2）；

a. Turn the body to the right, and to the left, then to the right again, hold the fan with the right hand and rotate inwards to the side of the right waist, at the same time, push the left palm forwards with the waist to the right, shift the body weight on to the left foot, the right toes up, looking in direction of the left palm(Fig.9-1;9-2).

（九）斜行拗步
9.Oblique Stance with Twist Step

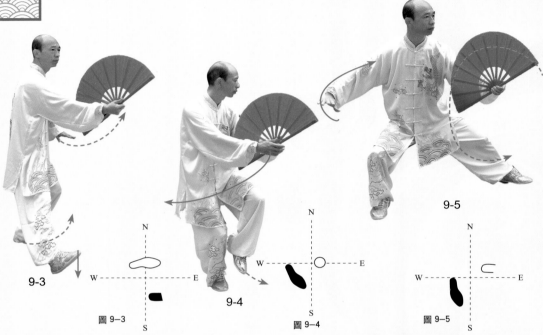

9-3

圖 9－3

9-4

圖 9－4

9-5

圖 9－5

2 身體左轉，右手內旋至右前方，立扇，左手收至左胯旁，同時提右腳向右前方上步，腳跟着地，目視右手方向（圖 9－3）；

b. Turn the body to the right, rotate the right hand inwards to in front of the right and, the fan upright, move the left hand to the side of the left hip, at the same time, lift the right foot and step forwards to the right, toes up, looking in direction of the right hand(Fig.9-3).

3 身體右轉，重心右移，提左腳向左前方擦出，同時左手接扇，立扇，右手收至右胯旁，目視左掌方向（圖 9－4；9－5）；

c. Turn the body to the right, shift the body weight to the right, lift the left foot and slide forwards to the left, at the same time, take the fan with the left hand, move the right hand to the side of the right hip, looking in direction of the left palm;(Fig.9-4;9-5).

（九）斜行拗步

9.Oblique Stance with Twist Step

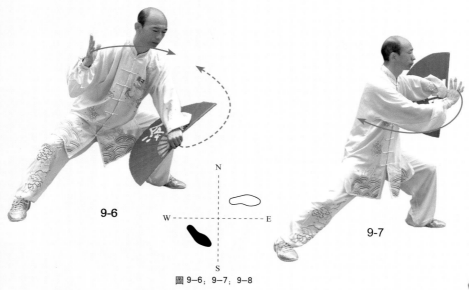

9-6

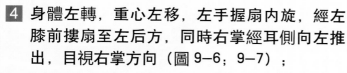

9-7

圖 9-6；9-7；9-8

4 身體左轉，重心左移，左手握扇內旋，經左膝前摟扇至左后方，同時右掌經耳側向左推出，目視右掌方向（圖 9-6；9-7）；

d. Turn the body to the left, shift the body weight to the left, hold the fan with the left hand and rotate inwards, and block through the front of the left knee to the left and rear, at the same time, push the right palm forwards through the side of the ear, looking in direction of the right palm. (Fig.9-6;9-7).

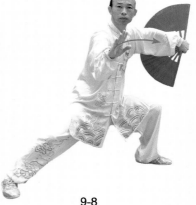

9-8

5 身體右轉，重心不移，成左弓步，右掌向右橫拉，立掌，目視右掌方向。（圖 9-8）；

d. Without shifting the body weight, turn the body to the right, adopt a left bow stance, pull the right palm horizontally to the right, palm upright, looking in direction of the right palm.(Fig.9-8).

（十）提收
10．Lift and retract

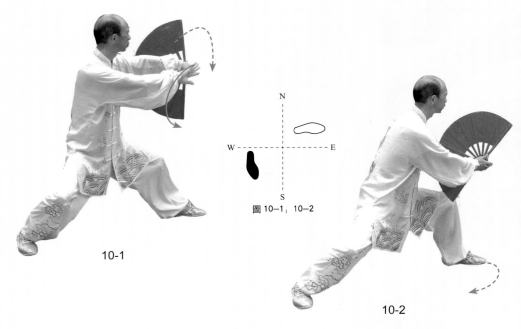

10-1

圖 10-1；10-2

10-2

---

1 身體左轉，重心右移，同時兩手相合，手背相對，目視兩掌方向（圖 10-1）；

a. Turn the body to the left, shift the body weight to the right, at the same time, palms come together, back to back, looking in direction of the palms (Fig.10-1).

2 重心左移，兩臂翻轉，兩手相合，左手握扇准備換至右手，目視兩掌方向（圖 10-2）；

b. Shift the body weight to the left, flip arms, palms facing each other, hold the fan with the left hand ready for a change to the right hand, looking in direction of the palms (Fig.10-2).

（十）提收
11.Lift and retract

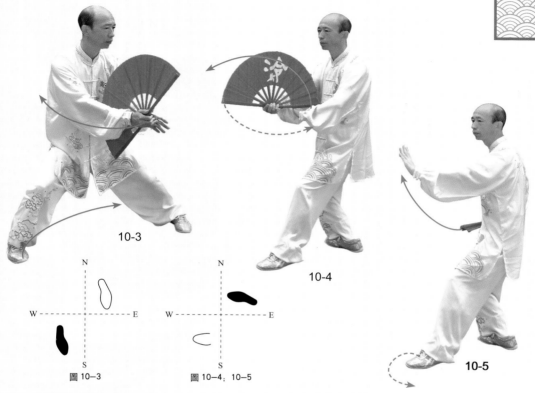

10-3

10-4

10-5

圖 10-3

圖 10-4；10-5

3 身體右轉，左腳內扣，右手接扇，目視兩掌方向（圖 10-3）；

c. Turn the body to the right, inner buckle the left foot, the right hand takes the fan, looking in direction of the palms (Fig.10-3).

4 身體繼續右轉，左掌內旋推出，順勢將扇收攏，右手握扇收至右跨旁，同時右腳后撤步，左腳提起再以腳尖着地，成虛步，目視左掌方向（圖 10-4；10-5）；

d. Without stopping, turn the body to the right, rotate the left palm inwards and push out, close the fan in the motion and hold the fan with the right hand and move to the side of the hip, at the same time, step back with the right foot, lift the left foot and rest on the toes to form an empty stance, looking in direction of the left palms (Fig.10-4;10-5).

（十）提收

11.Lift and retract

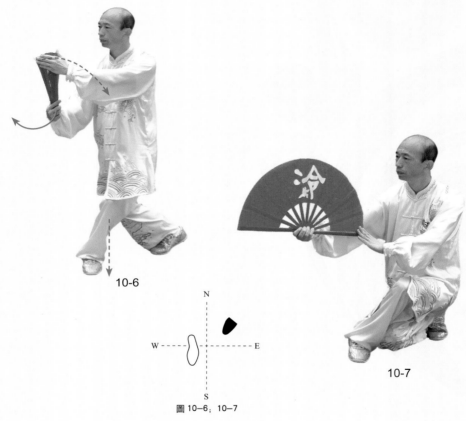

10-6

10-7

圖 10-6；10-7

5 身體左轉，重心右移，左腳踏實再外擺，兩腳交叉成歇步，左掌沿扇回收，順勢將扇打開，立扇，目視扇的方向（圖 10-6；10-7）；

e. Turn the body to the left, shift the body weight to the right, plant the left foot firmly, then swing it outwards, cross the feet to a cross-legged sitting stance, while retracting the left palm along with the fan, open the fan in the motion, the fan upright, Looking in direction of the fan(Fig.10-6;10-7).

（十一）雲手
11. Cloud Hands

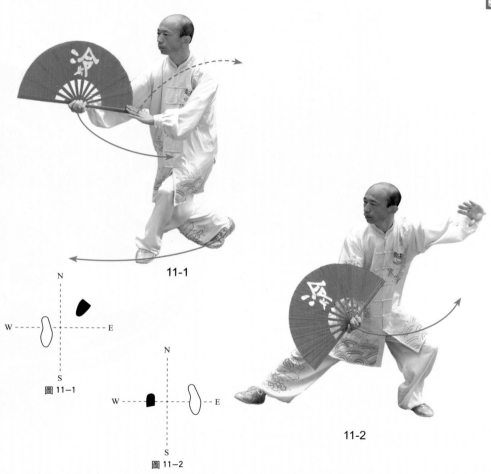

11-1

圖 11-1

圖 11-2

11-2

1 身體左轉，右腳向右擦出，兩手劃弧隨轉腰向左雲手，目視右腳方向（圖 11-1；11-2）；

a. Turn the body to the left, slide out the right foot to the right, rotate both hands with the waist to the left (left cloud hands), looking in direction of the right foot(Fig.11-1;11-2).

（十一）雲手
11．Cloud Hands

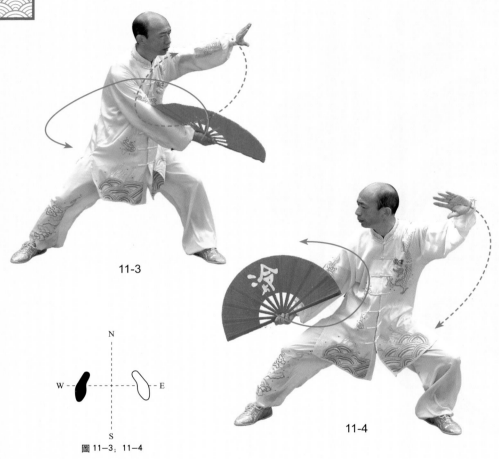

11-3

圖 11-3；11-4

11-4

2 身體右轉，兩手劃弧隨轉腰雲手，左手劃弧至左額斜上方，掌心向外，右手握扇劃弧至右膝上方，立扇，目視扇的方向（圖 11-3；11-4）；

b. Turn the body to the right, rotate both hands with the waist to cloud hands, draw the left hand in an arc to the upper left of the forehead, palm facing outwards, hold the fan with the right hand and draw in an arc to above the right knee, the fan upright, looking in direction of the fan(Fig.11-3;11-4).

（十一）雲手

11.Cloud Hands

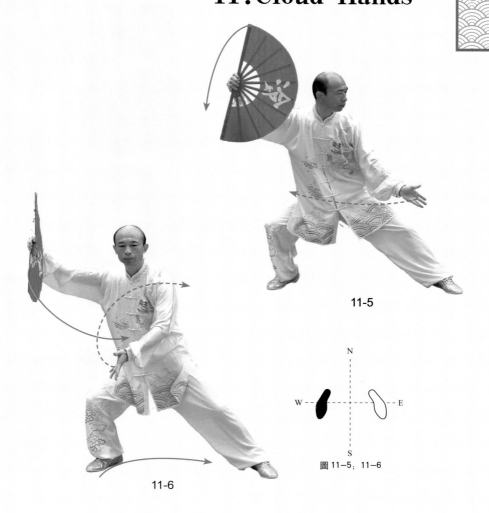

11-5

11-6

圖 11-5；11-6

3 身體左轉，兩手劃弧隨轉腰雲手，右手劃弧至右額斜上方，手心向內，左手劃弧至左膝上方，目視左手方向（圖 11-5）；

c. Turn the body to the left, rotate both hands with the waist to cloud hands, draw the right hand in an arc to the upper right of the forehead, palm facing inwards, draw the left hand in an arc to above the left knee, looking in direction of the left hand(Fig.11-5).

（十一）雲手
11. Cloud Hands

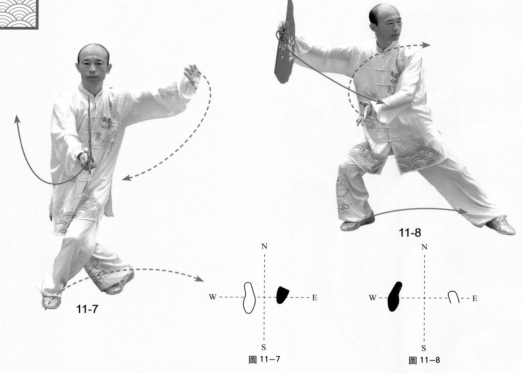

11-8

11-7

圖 11-7　　　　　圖 11-8

4 身體右轉再左轉，右腳從左腳後方插出，成叉步，同時兩手向左雲手，目視扇的方向（圖 11-6；11-7）；

d. Turn the body to the right, then to the left, step the right foot backwards from behind the left foot to adopt a cross-legged stance, at the same time, rotate both hands to the left (left cloud hands), looking in the direction of the fan(Fig.11-7).

5 身體右轉，重心右移，左腳向左擦出，同時兩手向右雲手，目視左腳方向（圖 11-8）；

e. Turn the body to the right, shift the body weight to the right, slide out the left foot to the left, at the same time, rotate both hands to the right (right cloud hands), looking in direction of the left foot(Fig.11-8).

（十一）雲手
11. Cloud Hands

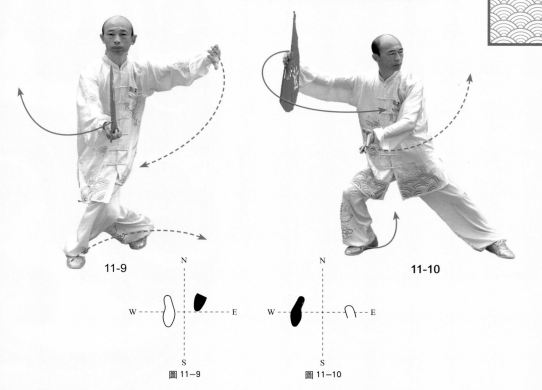

11-9

11-10

圖 11-9

圖 11-10

6 身體左轉，右腳從左腳後方插出，成叉步，同時兩手向左雲手，目視扇的方向（圖 11-9）；

f. Turn the body to the left, insert the right foot backwards from behind the left foot to adopt a cross-legged stance, at the same time, rotate the hands to the left (left cloud hands), looking in direction of the fan(Fig.11-9).

7 身體右轉，重心右移，左腳向左擦出，同時兩手向右雲手，目視左腳方向（圖 11-10）。

g. Turn the body to the right, shift the body weight to the right,slide out the left foot to the left, at the same time, rotate the hands to the right (right cloud hands), looking in direction of the left foot(Fig.11-10).

12

（十二）掩手肱捶

12. Hide Hand and Strike with Fist

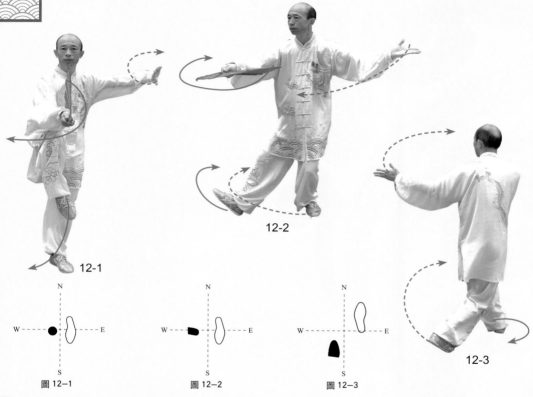

12-1

12-2

12-3

圖 12-1   圖 12-2   圖 12-3

1 身體左轉，重心左移，提右膝，右手舉扇，高與肩平，目視扇的方向（圖12-1）；

a. Turn the body to the left, shift the body weight to the left, lift the right knee, raise the fan with the right hand at shoulder-level, looking in direction of the fan(Fig.12-1).

2 身體右轉，右腳向右下落，右手握扇內旋，平扇，然后左腳向右后方扣腳下落，目視左手方向（圖12-2；12-3）；

b. Turn the body to the right, drop the right foot to the right, hold the fan with the right hand and rotate inwards flatly, then land the left foot buckled at the right rear, looking in direction of the left hand(Fig.12-2;12-3).

（十二）掩手肱捶
12.Hide Hand and Strike with Fist

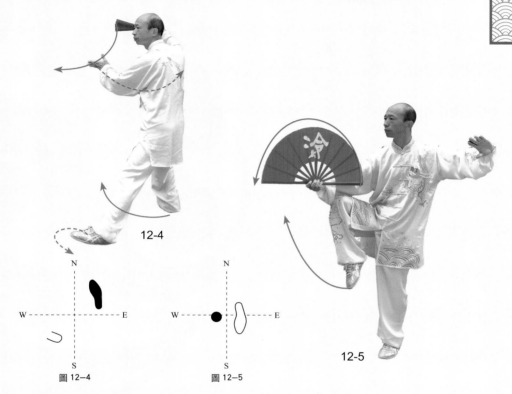

12-4

圖 12-4

12-5

圖 12-5

3 身體繼續右轉，右腳向右后撤步，左腳尖上翹，同時右手合扇，兩手向右后方平推，目視左腳方向（圖 12-4）；

c. Without stopping, turn the body to the right, step back with the right foot, the left toes up, at the same time, close the fan with the right hand, push both palms backwards flatly to the right, looking in direction of the left foot(Fig.12-4).

4 重心左移，提右膝，同時右手開扇，左手收至左側，掌心向外，高與肩平，目視扇的方向（圖 12-5）；

d. Shift the body weight to the left, lift the right knee, at the same time, open the fan with the right hand, move the left hand to the left side, palm facing outwards, at shoulder-level, looking in direction of the fan(Fig.12-5).

（十二）掩手肱捶
12.Hide Hand and Strike with Fist

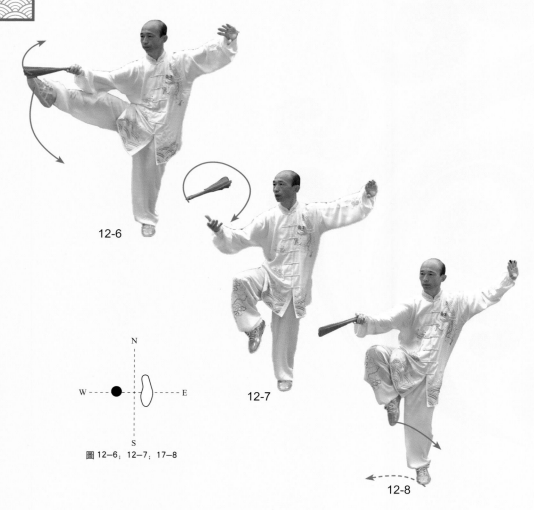

12-6

12-7

12-8

N
W — E
S

圖 12-6；12-7；17-8

5 右腳向前彈出，腳面繃平，同時右手合扇，然后拋扇，目視右手方向（圖 12-6；12-7；12-8）；

e. flick kick the right foot forwards, instep flattened, at the same time, close the fan with the right hand, then throw it, looking in direction of the right hand(Fig.12-6;12-7;12-8).

（十二）掩手肱捶

12.Hide Hand and Strike with Fist

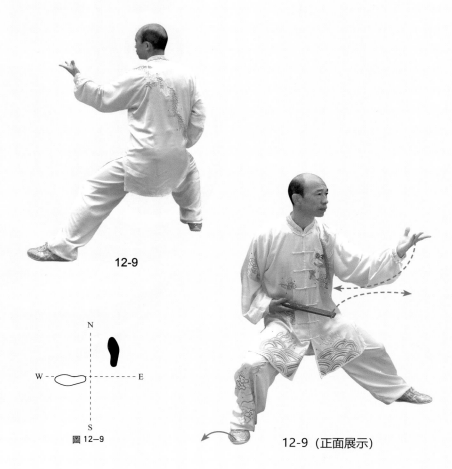

12-9

圖 12—9

12-9 （正面展示）

6 身體右轉，右腳下震在左腳內側，同時左腳向左前方擦出，右手握扇收至右腰側，左手至身體前方，掌心向上，目視左手方向（圖 12－9）；

f. Turn the body to the right, drop the right foot with a thud at inside of the left foot, at the same time, slide the left foot forwards to the left, move the fan with the right hand to the side of the waist, move the left hand to the front of the body, palm facing up, looking in direction of the left hand(Fig.12-9).

（十二）掩手肱捶
12.Hide Hand and Strike with Fist

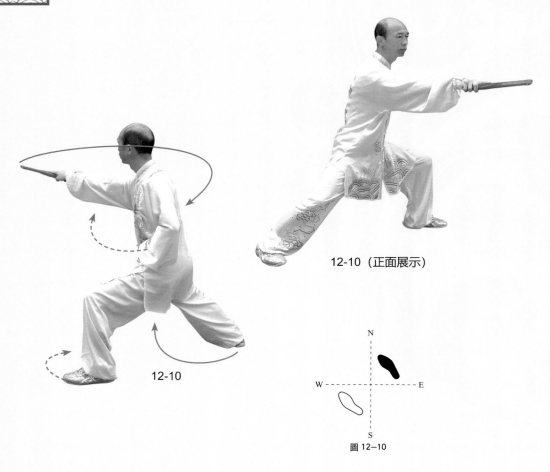

12-10 （正面展示）

12-10

圖 12-10

7 身體左轉，重心左移，右腳蹬地，以腰為軸，右手螺旋向前衝擊，同時左肘向後頂肘，目視右手方向（圖 12-10）。

g. Turn the body to the left, shift the body weight to the left, thrust the right foot on the ground, with the waist as axis, punch the right hand spirally forwards, at the same time, jab the left elbow backwards, looking in direction of the right hand (Fig.12-10).

（十三）穿心肘
13. Pierce Elbow

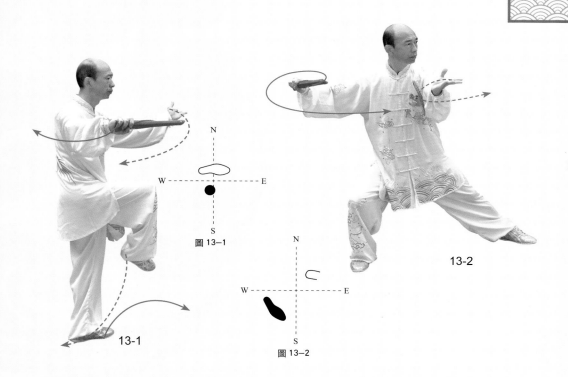

圖 13−1

13-1

13-2

圖 13−2

1 身體右轉，提右腳以左腳腳掌爲軸向右轉 180 度，兩手隨轉腰向右平帶，目視兩手方向（圖 13−1）；

a.Turn the body to the right, lift the right foot, turn the body 180°to the right with the sole of the left foot as the axis, with the rotation of the waist, pull both hands flatly to the right , looking in direction of the hands(Fig.13-1).

2 右腳下震于左腳內側，同時左腳向左擦出，兩手向右推出，目視左腳方向（圖 13−2）；

b. drop the right foot with a thud at inside of the left foot, at the same time, slide out the left foot to the left, push both hands to the right, looking in direction of the left foot(Fig.13-2).

（十三）穿心肘
13. Pierce Elbow

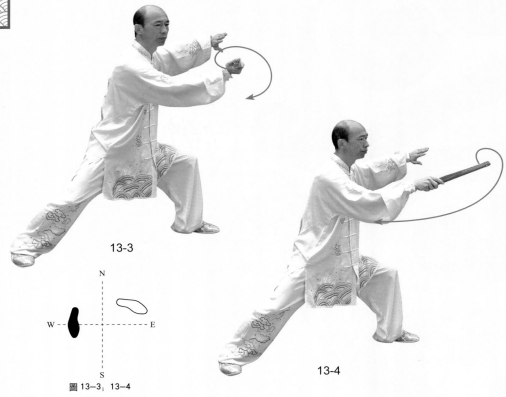

13-3

圖 13−3；13−4

13-4

3 身體左轉，重心左移，兩手順時針劃弧，右手握扇向左平推，左手至左肩側，掌心向外，目視右手方向（圖 13−3）；

c. Turn the body to the left, shift the body weight to the left, draw hands clockwise in an arc, hold the fan with the right hand and push to the left flatly, the left hand to the side of the left shoulder, palm facing outwards, looking in direction of the right hand(Fig.13-3).

4 右手逆時針翻轉，將扇收至右手臂下側，目視右手方向（圖 13−4；13−5）；

d. flip the right hand counterclockwise, tuck the fan under the right arm, looking in direction of the right hand(Fig.13-4;13-5).

（十三）穿心肘

13. Pierce Elbow

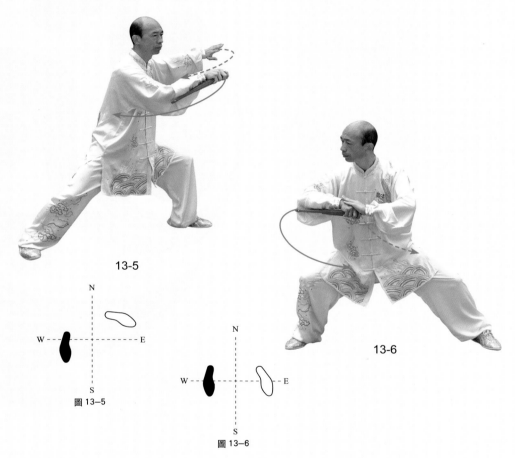

13-5

圖 13-5

13-6

圖 13-6

5 重心右移，左手附于右手握扇位置，向右頂肘發力，同時兩腳向右滑步，目視右肘方向（圖 13-6）。

e. shift the body weight to the right, the left hand touches the position of the right hand fan grip, the right elbow exerts a force and jab, while the feet sliding to the right, looking in direction of the elbow(Fig.13-6).

（十四） 擺蓮腳
14. Lotus Kick

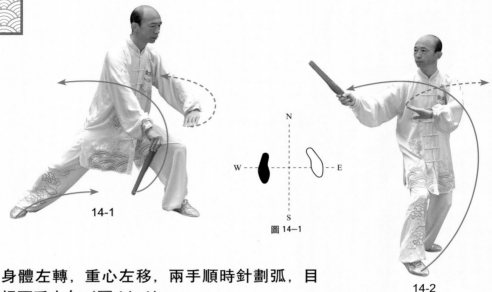

14-1

圖 14—1

14-2

1 身體左轉，重心左移，兩手順時針劃弧，目
視兩手方向（圖 14—1）；

a. Turn the body to the left, shift the body weight
to the left, rotate both arms clockwise in an arc,
looking in direction of the hands(Fig.14-1).

2 身體右轉，兩手劃弧收至右肩側，目視右
手方向（圖 14—2）；

b. Turn the body to the right, rotate both arms
to the side of the right shoulder, looking in
direction of the right hand(Fig.14-2).

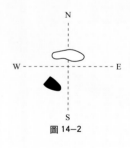

圖 14—2

3 提右腳，自左向右做扇形擺幅，同時兩掌擊拍腳面，目視拍腳方向（圖
14—3）。

c. Lift the right foot, swing from left to right in a fan-shaped, at the same
time, slap the foot instep with both palms, looking in direction of the slapping
foot(Fig.14-3).

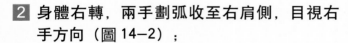

（十五）雀地龍
15. Dragon Dives to Ground

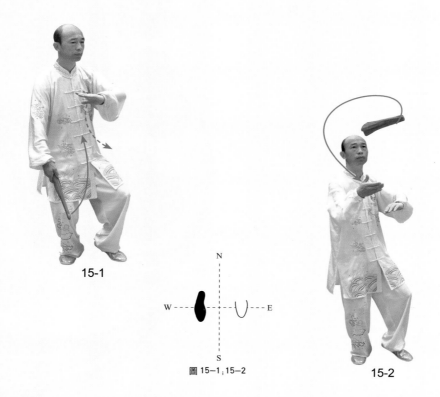

15-1

圖 15—1；15—2

15-2

1 右腳下震于左腳內側，右手握扇至右膝上方，左手收至胸前，目視前方（圖15—1）；

a.Drop the right foot with a thud at inside of the left foot, hold the fan with the right hand and move to above the right knee, move the left hand to in front of the chest, looking straight ahead(Fig.15-1).

2 拋扇后接扇，兩手劃弧向右至右肩前，同時左腳向左擦出，目視左腳方向（圖15—2）；

b.Throw the fan, then catch it, draw the hands in an arc to the right to in front of the right shoulder, at the same time, slide out the left foot to the left, looking in direction of the left foot(Fig.15-2).

（十五）雀地龍

15. Dragon Dives to Ground

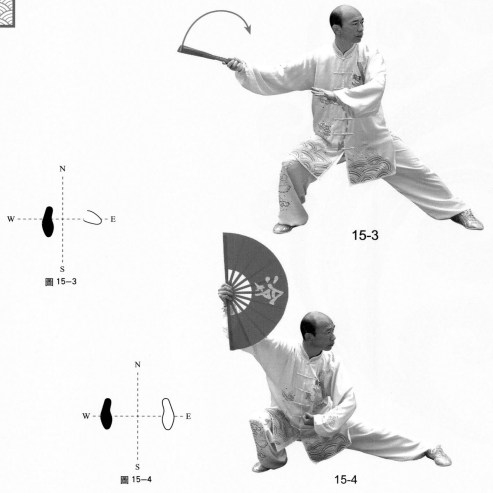

15-3

圖 15-3

15-4

圖 15-4

3 右手開扇，左手變拳收至腹前，同時身體下蹲成僕步，目視左前方（15-3；15-4）

c. Open the fan with the right hand, clench the left fist and move to in front of the abdomen, at the same time, squat down into a crouch stance, looking forwards to the left(Fig.15-3；15-4).

（十六）金鷄獨立

16．Golden Rooster Stands on one Leg

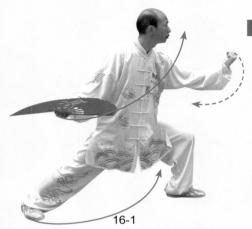

16-1

1 左腿前弓，右腿后蹬，變弓步，左拳前穿，右手握扇收至右腰側，目視左拳方向（圖16−1）；

a. Arch the left foot forwards and press the right leg backwards on the ground to form a bow stance, pierce the left fist forwards, hold the fan with the right hand and move to the side of the right waist, looking in direction of the left fist(Fig.16-1).

2 右手經腰側向上穿扇至頭頂，手心向前，左臂內旋變掌，下按至左胯旁，同時提右膝，腳尖下垂，目視前方（圖16−2）。

b. The right hand pierces the fan through beside the waist up to the top of the head, palm facing forwards, unclench the fist while rotating the left arm inwards, press the palm down to the side of the left hip, at the same time, lift the right knee with toes down, looking straight ahead(Fig.16-2).

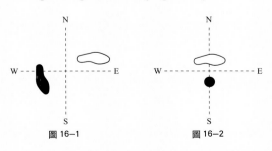

圖16−1　　　圖16−2

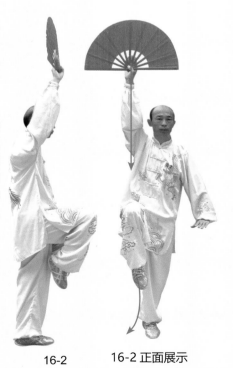

16-2　　　16-2 正面展示

（十六）金鷄獨立

16.Golden Rooster Stands on one Leg

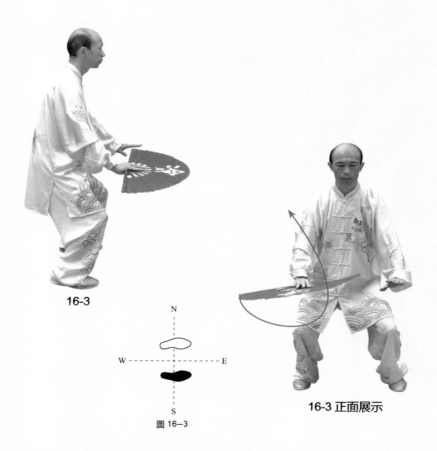

16-3

圖 16－3

16-3 正面展示

3 右腳下震至左腳內側，與肩同寬，同時右手握扇向下拍扇，目視前方（圖 16－3）；

a. drop the right foot with a thud at inside of the left foot, shoulder -width, at the same time, hold the fan with the right hand and slap it down, looking straight ahead(Fig.16-3).

（十七）翻花舞袖

17. Turn over flowers and flip sleeves

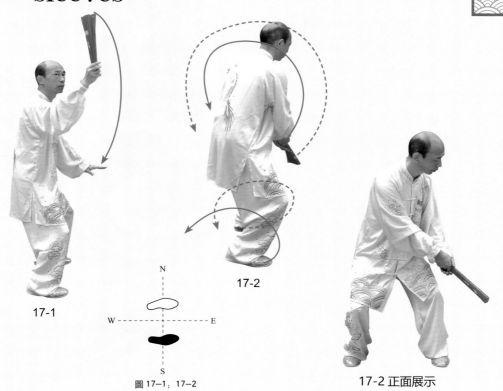

17-1

17-2

N

W———————E

S

圖 17-1；17-2

17-2 正面展示

1 身體右轉，順勢收扇，目視右手方向（圖 17-1）；

b. While turning the body to the right, close the fan in the motion, looking in direction of the right hand(Fig.17-1).

2 身體左轉，兩手逆時針翻轉，右手將扇交給左手，同時提右膝，目視左掌方向（圖 17-2）；

c. Turn the body to the left, flip both hands counterclockwise, the right hand hands over the fan to the left hand, at the same time, lift the right knee, looking in direction of the left palm(Fig.17-2).

（十七）翻花舞袖

17. Turn over flowers and flip sleeves

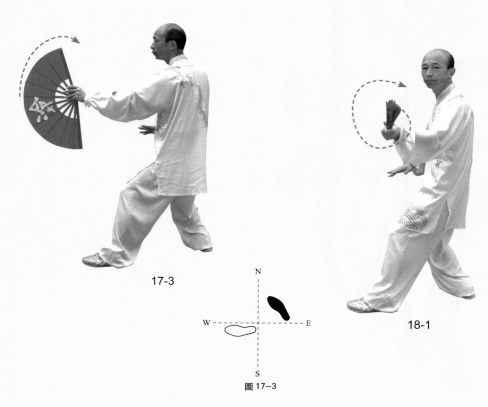

17-3

圖 17-3

18-1

4 身體向身后跳轉（180°），右腳先着地，左腳在左前方，重心在右腳，同時兩手順時針掄劈，左掌在前，右手順勢開扇，目視左掌方向（圖 17-3）。

d. Jumps up and turn the body 180°backwards, the right foot drops down to the ground first, and the left foot is in front of the left, the body weight is on the right foot, at the same time, both hands swing in a clockwise chop, the left palm in front, the right hand opens the fan in a downward motion, looking in direction of the left palm(Fig.17-3).

（十八）海底翻花
18.Flip the ocean waves

18

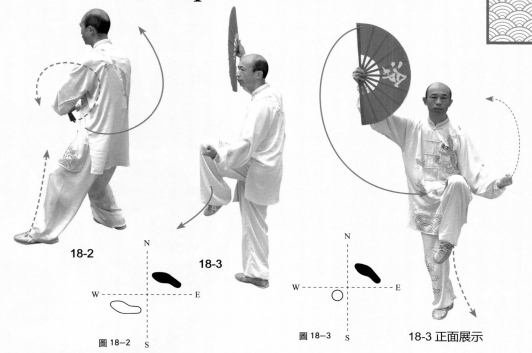

18-2

18-3

圖 18-2

圖 18-3

18-3 正面展示

1 身體左轉，左手順勢收扇，目視左手方向（圖 18-1）；

a. Turn the body to the left, the left hand closes the fan in the motion, looking in direction of the left hand(Fig.18-1).

2 身體右轉，左手將扇交給右手，目視右手方向（圖 18-2）；

b. Turn the body to the right, the left hand hands over the fan to the right hand, looking in direction of the right hand(Fig.18-2).

3 身體左轉，同時提左膝，左臂逆時針翻轉，砸于左膝外側，右手開扇向左向上發力，目視前方（圖 18-3）。

c. Turn the body to the left, at the same time, lift the left knee, turn the left arm counterclockwise and chop at the outside of the left knee, open the fan with the right hand while exerting a force upwards to the left, looking straight ahead(Fig.18-3).

（十九）二起腳
19. jump with double kicks

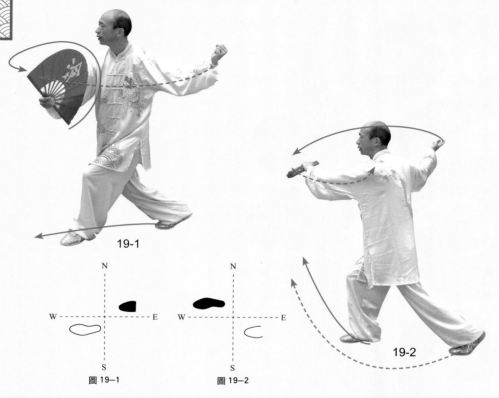

19-1

圖 19-1

19-2

圖 19-2

1 身體左轉，左腳向前落地，腳尖外擺，兩手隨轉腰向左劃弧，目視前方（圖 19-1）；

a. Turn the body to the left, drop the left foot forward on the ground, swing the toes outwards, and draw both arms in an arc to the left with the rotation of the waist, looking straight ahead(Fig.19-1).

2 身體右轉，右腳上步，右手順勢收扇交給左手，右手變掌舉至右肩側（圖 19-2）；

b. Turn the body to the right, step the right foot forwards, the right hand closes the fan in the motion and hands over to the left hand, unclench the right fist and hold up the palm to the side of right shoulder(Fig.19-2).

（十九）二起腳
19. jump with double kicks

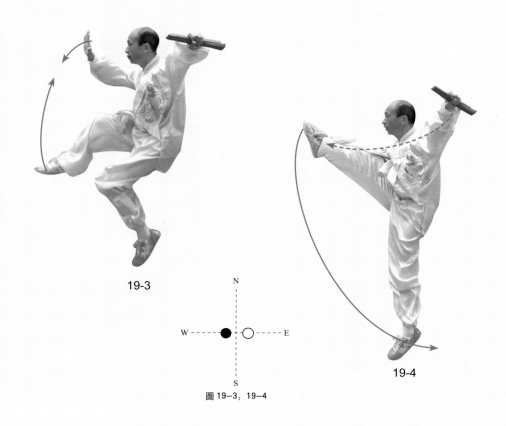

19-3

19-4

圖 19-3；19-4

3 左腳提膝，右腳緊跟上踢，腳面繃平，左手劃弧至左側，掌心向下，右掌經耳側擊拍腳面，目視右掌方向（圖 19-3；19-4）。

c. Lift the left knee, followed by kicking the right foot upwards, instep flattened, draw the left hand in an arc to the left side, palm facing down, the right palm passes the side of the ear and slaps on the instep, looking in direction of the right palm(Fig.19-3;19-4).

（二十）雙震腳

20. Thuds with both feet

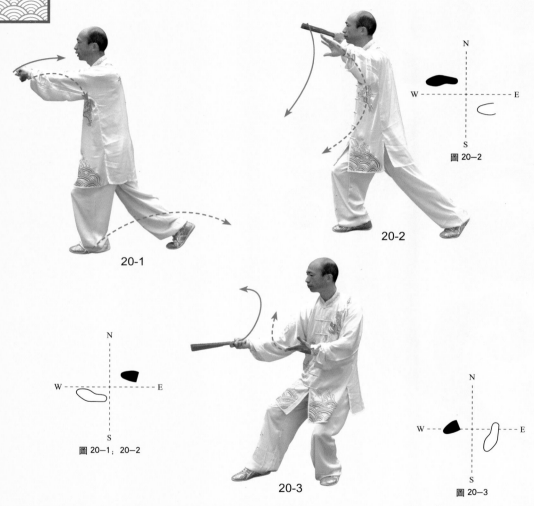

圖 20—2

20-2

20-1

圖 20—1；20—2

20-3

圖 20—3

1 左腳落地，向后跳兩步，右腳在前，同時左手將扇交給右手，目視前方（圖 20—1；20—2；20—3）；

a. The left foot drops on the ground, then jump two steps backwards, the right foot at front, at the same time, the left hand hands over the fan to the right hand, looking straight ahead(Fig.20-1;20-2;20-3).

（二十）雙震腳

20. Thuds with both feet

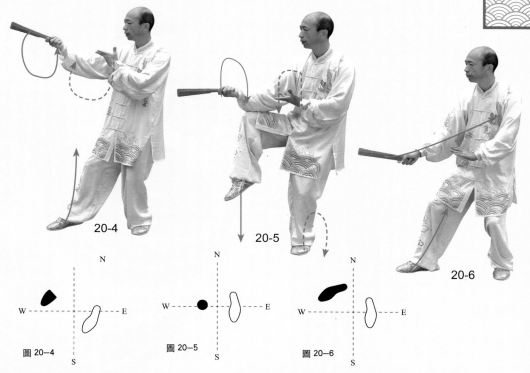

20-4

20-5

20-6

圖 20-4 圖 20-5 圖 20-6

2 兩手合勁外旋上托，右手在前，再內旋下按，目視兩掌方向（圖 20-4）；

b. Rotate both hands outwards with a strength of closing together and hold upwards, then press down with inwards rotations, the right hand in front, looking in direction of palms(Fig.20-4).

3 兩手外旋上托，同時兩腳上跳，右腳先起，目視兩掌方向（圖 20-5）；

c. Rotate both hands outwards and hold upward while jumping up both feet, right foot first, looking in direction of palms(Fig.20-5).

4 兩腳下震，左腳先落，重心在左腳，同時兩手內旋下按，目視兩掌方向（圖 20-6）。

d. Both feet drop down to the ground with thuds, left foot down first, the body weight is on the left foot, at the same time,press down hands with inwards rotations, looking in direction of the palms(Fig.20-6).

（二十一）玉女穿梭

21.Jade Maiden Working Shuttles

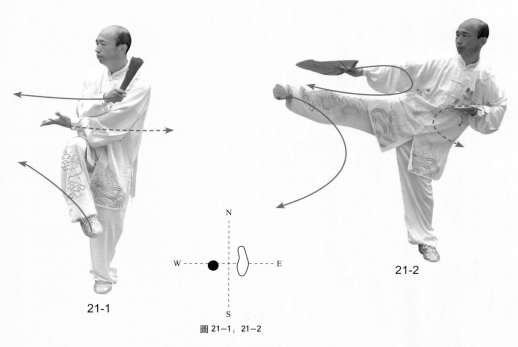

21-1

21-2

圖 21-1；21-2

1 身體左轉，兩手相合收于胸前，同時提右膝，目視前方（圖 21-1）；

a. Turn the body to the left, close both hands together and move to in front of the chest. At the same time, lift the right knee, looking straight ahead(Fig.21-1).

2 身體繼續左轉，右腳以腳外沿向右側踹，同時右手向右開扇發力，左手屈臂向后頂肘，目視右手方向（圖 21-2）；

b. Without stopping, turn the body to the left, kick the right foot with an outer edge of the right foot to the right side,at the same time, open the fan with the right hand to the right while exerting a force, bend the left elbow and jab it backwards, looking in direction of the right hand(Fig.21-2).

（二十一）玉女穿梭

21.Jade Maiden Working Shuttles

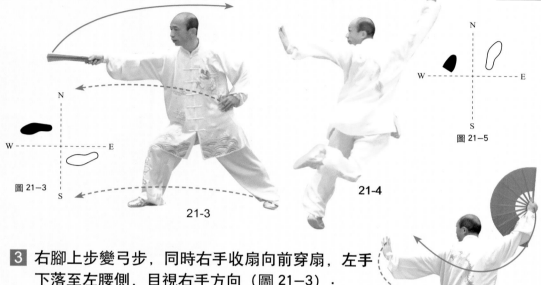

圖 21-3

21-3

21-4

圖 21-5

21-5

3 右腳上步變弓步，同時右手收扇向前穿扇，左手下落至左腰側，目視右手方向（圖 21-3）；

c. Step the right foot forwards to a bow stance, at the same time, retrieve the fan with the right hand and pierce it forwards, move the left hand down to the side of the left waist, looking in direction of the right hand.(Fig.21-3).

4 身體右轉，右腳蹬地，向前轉身跳兩步，右腳從左腳后側插出變叉步，同時左掌向前推出，力達掌根，右手開扇在右肩上方，目視左掌方向（圖 21-4；21-5）。

d. Turn the body to the right, thrust the right foot on the ground and jump two steps forwards with the turning of the body, insert the right foot backwards from behind the left foot to adopt a cross-legged stance, at the same time, push the left palm forwards, the point of force reaching the base of the palm, the right hand opens the fan at above the right shoulder, looking in direct of the left palm(Fig.21-4;21-5).

（二十二）當頭炮
22. cannon attack

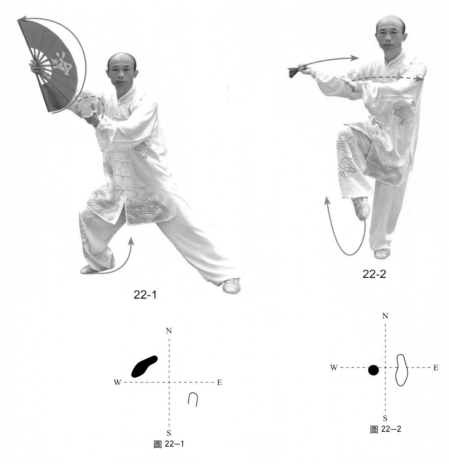

22-1

22-2

圖 22−1

圖 22−2

1 身體右轉，兩手對轉腰劃弧，右手順勢收扇，同時提左腳，目視前方（圖 22−1；22−2）；

a. Turn the body to the right, rotate both hands with the waist in an arc, the right hand closes the fan in the motion, at the same time, lift the left foot, looking straight ahead(Fig.22-1；22-2).

（二十二）當頭炮

22. cannon attack

22

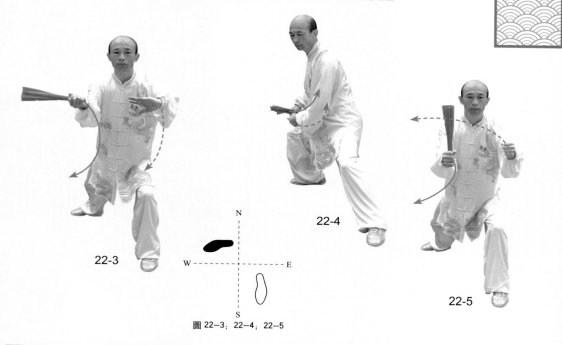

22-4

22-3

22-5

N

W — — — — — — E

S

圖 22-3；22-4；22-5

2 右腳向右后撤步，同時兩手向前平推，目視前方（圖 22-3）；

b. Step the right foot backwards to the right, at the same time, push both hands levelly forwards, looking straight ahead(Fig.22-3).

3 身體右轉，兩手劃弧收至腹前，左掌變拳，目視兩手方向（圖 22-4）；

c. Turn the body to the right, draw both hands in an arc to in front of the abdomen, clench the left fist, looking in direction of the hands(Fig.22-4).

4 身體左轉，兩手向前擊出，左拳拳眼向上，右手握扇，立扇，目視前方（圖 22-5）。

d. Turn the body to the left, punch forwards with both hands, the left fist eye facing up, the right hand holding the fan, upright, looking straight ahead(Fig.22-5).

（二十三）金剛搗碓
23.Guardian Pounds Mortar

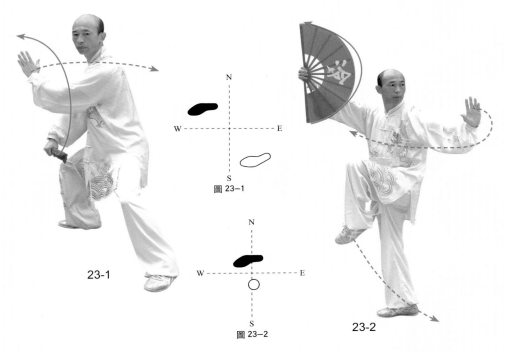

圖 23-1

23-1

圖 23-2

23-2

1 身體右轉，左拳變掌向右撥掌，右手握扇收至腹前，目視前方（圖 23-1）；

a. Turn the body to the right, unclench the left fist and pull it to the right, move the right hand with the fan to in front of the abdomen, looking straight ahead(Fig.23-1).

2 身體左轉，右手順勢開扇，左手向左推掌，同時提左膝，目視左手方向（圖 23-2）；

b. Turn the body to the left, open the fan with the right hand in the motion , push the left palm to the left, at the same time, lift the left knee, looking in direction of the left hand(Fig.23-2).

（二十三）金剛搗碓

23.Guardian Pounds Mortar

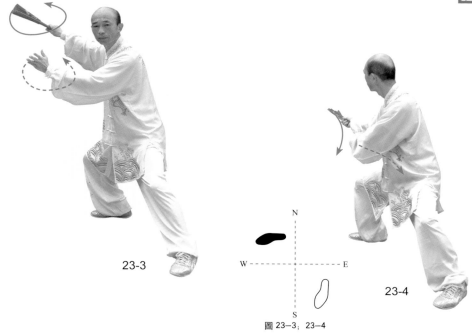

23-3

23-4

圖 23-3，23-4

3 左腳向左前方擦出，右手順勢收扇，左手劃弧至右肩前，目視左前方（圖 23-3）；

c. Slide the left foot forwards to the left, open the fan with the right hand in the motion, draw the left hand in an arc to in front of the right shoulder, looking forwards to the left(Fig.23-3).

4 身體左轉再右轉，重心左移再右移，兩手順時針旋轉，目視兩掌方向（圖 23-4）；

d. Turn the body to the left, then to the right, shift the body weight to the left, then to the right, rotate both hands clockwise, looking in direction of palms(Fig.23-4).

（二十三） 金剛搗碓
23.Guardian Pounds Mortar

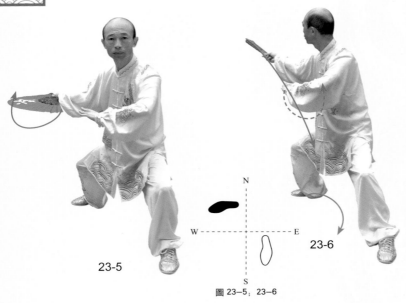

23-5

W ─── E
N
S

23-6

圖 23-5；23-6

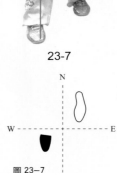

23-7

W ─── E
N
S

圖 23-7

5 身體左轉，重心左移，左手屈肘向前頂肘，同時右手開扇，目視左前方（圖 23-5）；

e. Turn the body to the left, shift the body weight to the left, bend the left arm and jab the elbow forwards, at the same time, open the fan with the right hand, looking forwards to the left(Fig.23-5).

6 右腳走內弧向前上步，腳尖點地成虛步，同時左手向前撩掌，右手隨右腳向前和左掌相搭，左掌搭於右前臂，目視右掌方向（圖 23-6；23-7）；

f. Step the right foot forwards in an inward arc, resting on tips of toes to form an empty stance, at the same time, flick the left palm forwards, flick the right hand forward to meet with the left palm, the left palm rests on the right forearm, looking in direction of the right palm(Fig.23-6;23-7).

（二十三）金剛搗碓

23.Guardian Pounds Mortar

23

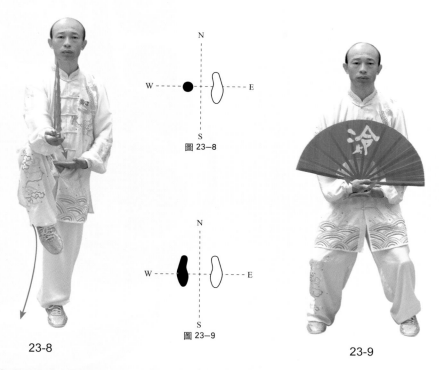

圖 23－8

圖 23－9

23-8

23-9

7 右掌變拳微下沉再上舉，與鼻同高，左掌收至腹前，掌心向上，同時提右膝，高過水平，腳尖下垂，目視前方（圖 23－8）；

g. Clench the right fist, sink down slightly, then raise to nose -level, move the left palm to in front of the abdomen, palm facing up, at the same time, lift the right knee, higher than level, toes facing down, looking straight ahead(Fig.23-8).

8 右腳下震，與肩同寬，重心偏左腳，兩腳平行，同時右手砸於左掌上，目視前方（圖 23－9）。

h. Drop the right foot with a thud, shoulder- width apart, the body weight slightly to the left, feet parallel, at the same time, pound the back of the right hand onto the left palm, looking straight ahead(Fig.23-9).

24

（二十四）收勢
24. Closing form

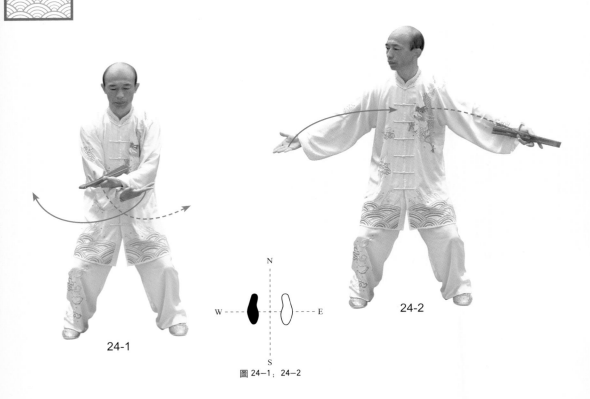

24-1

24-2

圖 24—1；24—2

1 身體微右轉再左轉，重心先右移再左移，先收扇換左手握扇，目視兩手方向（圖 24—1）；

a. Turn the body to the right slightly, then to the left, shift the body weight to the right, then to the left, close the fan, the left hand takes it, looking in direct of the hands(Fig.24-1).

2 兩手經腰側向兩邊分開，目視前方（圖 24—2）；

b. separate the hands sideways by passing through the sides of the waist, looking straight ahead(Fig.24-2).

（二十四） 收勢
24. Closing form

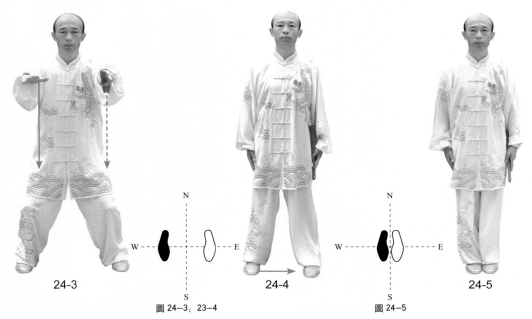

24-3   24-4   24-5

圖 24−3；23−4   圖 24−5

3 兩手劃弧收至前方，與肩同高，手心向下，目視前方（圖 24−3）；

c. Draw both hands in an arc to the front at shoulder-height, palms facing down, looking straight ahead(Fig.24-3).

4 鬆肩墜肘，兩臂下落至兩腿外側，目視前方（圖 24−4）；

d. Relax shoulders and drop elbows, drop the arms at outside of the legs, looking straight ahead(Fig.24-4).

5 左腳收至右腳內側，并步還原，目視前方（圖 24−5）。

e. Move the left foot to the inside of the right foot with feet together, to their original stance, looking straight ahead(Fig.24-5).

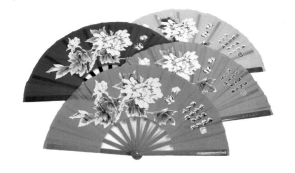

【太極扇】

武術/廣場舞/表演扇

可訂制LOGO

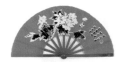

紅色牡丹

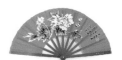

粉色牡丹

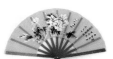

黃色牡丹

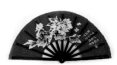

紫色牡丹

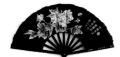

黑色牡丹

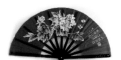

藍色牡丹

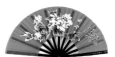

綠色牡丹

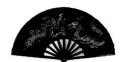

黑色龍鳳

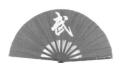

紅色武字

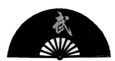

黑色武字

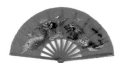

紅色龍鳳

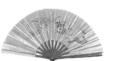

金色龍鳳

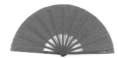

純紅色

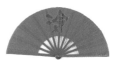

紅色冷字

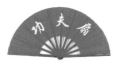

紅色功夫扇

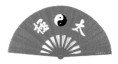

紅色太極

打開淘寶天貓APP

掃碼進店

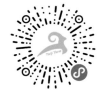

微信掃一掃

進入小程序購買

【武術/表演/比賽/專業太極鞋】

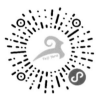

打開淘寶天貓
掃碼進店

微信掃一掃
進入小程序購買

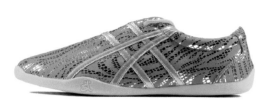

正紅色【升級款】
XF001 正紅

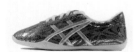

藍色【經典款】
XF8008-2 藍

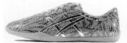

黃色【經典款】
XF8008-2 黃色

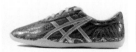

紫色【經典款】
XF8008-2 紫色

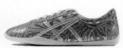

正紅色【經典款】
XF8008-2 正紅

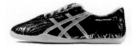

黑色【經典款】
XF8008-2 黑

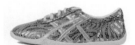

綠色【經典款】
XF8008-2 綠

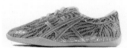

桔紅色【經典款】
XF8008-2 桔紅

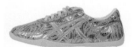

粉色【經典款】
XF8008-2 粉

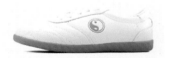

XF2008B（太極圖）白

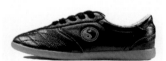

XF2008B（太極圖）黑

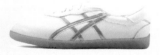

XF2008-2 白

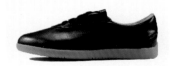

XF2008-3 黑

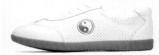

5634 白

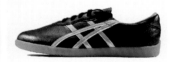

XF2008-2 黑

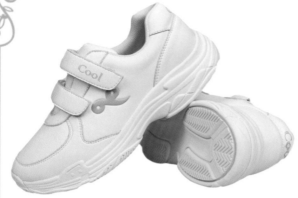

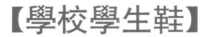
【學校學生鞋】

多種款式選擇・男女同款

可定制logo

香港及海外掃碼購買

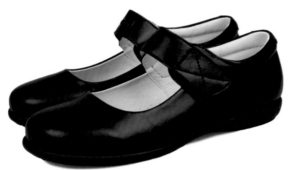

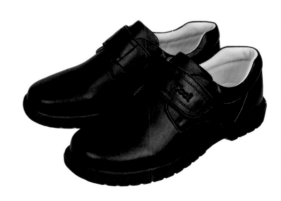

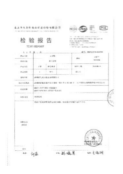 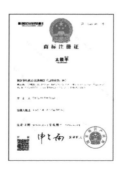

檢測報告　　　　商品注冊證

打開淘寶天貓APP

掃碼進店

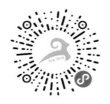
微信掃一掃

進入小程序購買

香港國際武術總會裁判員、教練員培訓班
常年舉辦培訓

　　香港國際武術總會培訓中心是經過香港政府注册、香港國際武術總會認證的培訓部門。爲傳承中華傳統文化、促進武術運動的開展，加强裁判員、教練員隊伍建設，提高武術裁判員、教練員綜合水平，以進一步規範科學訓練爲目的，選拔、培養更多的作風硬、業務精、技術好的裁判員、教練員團隊。特開展常年培訓，報名人數每達到一定數量，即舉辦培訓班。

報名條件：熱愛武術運動，思想作風正派，敬業精神强，有較高的職業道德，男女不限。

培訓內容：1.規則培訓；2.裁判法；3.技術培訓。考核內容：1.理論、規則考試；2.技術考核；3.實際操作和實踐（安排實際比賽實習）。經考核合格者頒發結業證書。培訓考核優秀者，將會錄入香港國際武術總會人才庫，有機會代表參加重大武術比賽，并提供宣傳、推廣平臺。

聯系方式
深圳：13143449091（微信同號）
　　　13352912626（微信同號）
香港：0085298500233（微信同號）

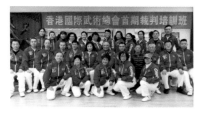

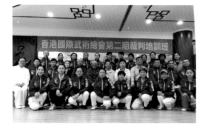

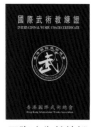

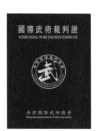

國際武術教練證　　　國際武術裁判證

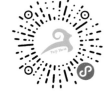

微信掃一掃

進入小程序

香港國際武術總會第三期裁判、教練培訓班

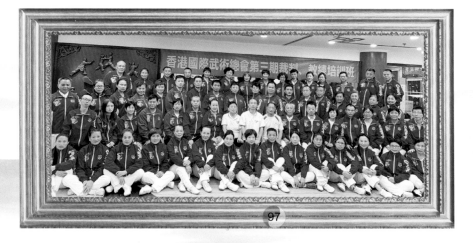

打開淘寶APP

掃碼進店

【出版各種書籍】

冷先鋒

申請書號>設計排版>印刷出品

>市場推廣

港澳台各大書店銷售

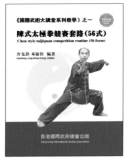

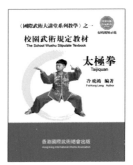

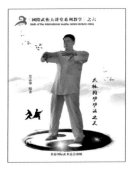

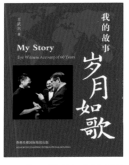

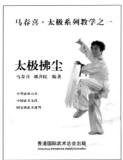

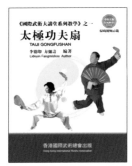

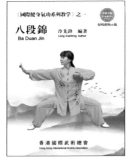

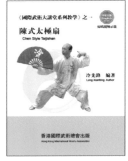

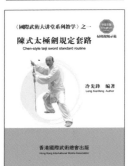

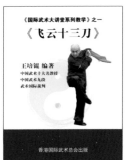

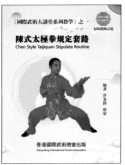

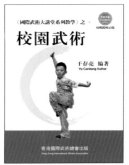

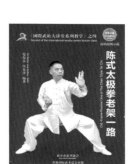
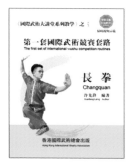
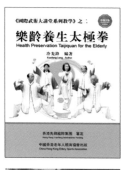
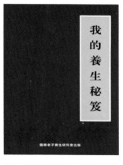
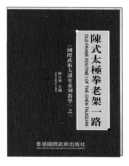
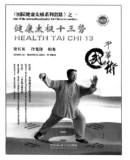
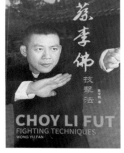
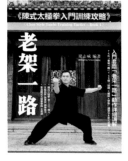
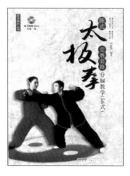
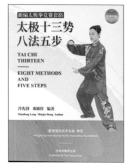
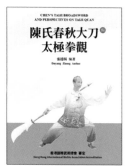
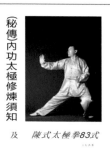
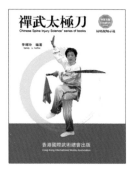
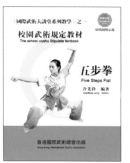
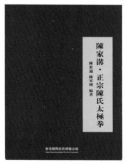
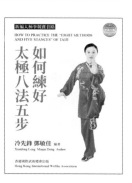

國際武術大講堂系列教學之一
《陳式太極扇》

香港先鋒國際集團 審定

太極羊集團　贊助

香港國際武術總會有限公司 出版

香港聯合書刊物流有限公司 發行

代理商：台灣白象文化事業有限公司

書號：ISBN 978-988-75077-5-8

香港地址：香港九龍彌敦道 525 -543 號寶寧大廈 C 座 412 室

電話：00852-95889723 \91267932

深圳地址：深圳市羅湖區紅嶺中路 2018 號建設集團大廈 B 座 20A

電話：0755-25950376\13352912626

台灣地址：401 台中市東區和平街 228 巷 44 號

電話：04-22208589

印刷：香港嘉越發展有限公司

印次：2021 年 3 月第一次印刷

印數：5000 冊

總編輯：冷先鋒

責任編輯：鄧敏佳

責任印制：冷修寧

版面設計：明栩成

圖片攝影：張念斯

網站：https:// www.taijixf.com　　https://taijiyanghk.com

Email: lengxianfeng@yahoo.com.hk